By

Oman Evans

Contents

Preface

A dilemma we face with understanding the Book of Mormon and hence Nephi, one of the main protagonists is that it is too commonplace. Who hasn't heard of the Book of Mormon? The book is responsible for a Broadway show that has been continuously running and attracting audiences for over a decade. We have all heard something about it and, yet, who really has the time to understand the hype? The Book of Mormon is over 500 pages long. I feel for those who want perhaps a basic understanding of the material but can't commit to dozens of hours of study. What is one to do? I also feel for those who are interested in the Latter-day Saint faith and feel they have years of catch-up to do. With this in mind, I hope to help one realize what the hype is about.

I hope to make evident some of the effects a lifelong student of the Book of Mormon and the Bible undergoes. Some of those students have been motivated to learn new languages and some have left homes for years on multiple occasions. Why? What is driving those people?

This would be easiest performed via a character analysis of Nephi and a portrait of the world Nephi lived in. Nephi is the first author in the Book of Mormon, and we have about 100 pages of unabridged text from him. This is not an official view of Nephi by any measure.

A quick note about the ground rules here: I take most statements from Nephi at face value. That is to say, this is not a debate regarding evidence. There are hundreds of posts curated and indexed on *BookofMormonCentral.org* or

EvidenceCentral.org and, other places if one is interested in those conversations. For me, I don't think debates about the veracity of the Book of Mormon are helpful. If the Book of Mormon is true, then surely Ezekiel's words apply. Ezekiel talked about the long-dead bones of the remains of Israel hearing the word of the Lord and rising from the dead. They rose with strength comparable to an army and gathered to their homelands. It was only **then** that they knew it was the Lord who had risen them. If that is how an all-powerful deity uses the Word, then that is how it works. I believe debates over the veracity of the Book of Mormon are futile at best.

I will bring history to the table when it helps us understand Nephi. I'll also go over a wide range of topics but will only be able to hit the peaks of each wave, so to speak.

Chapter 1

Who is Nephi?

What sort of world did Nephi live in? What was his life like? What did he learn? Is there a mantra or code that drives his successes and failures?

Nephi seems to be well-educated and literate. Estimates suggest literacy was not common in his time, and this indicates Nephi's social status is likely in the ancient version of today's mid-to-upper class. He lived around 600 BCE in the areas surrounding Jerusalem. That was about a decade before the destruction of the Kingdom of Judah. Although the city was in decline, Nephi reveals to us no sense of desperation. He depicts Jerusalem as a great city and indicates that its people did not believe that it could be destroyed.

Nephi knew both Egyptian and Hebrew. If his education was not purely academic, his family's vocation required him to be bilingual. Occupations that may have required such knowledge include scribes, lawyers, and traveling merchants.

We later learn Nephi's family desired to leave Jerusalem covertly. This suggests that they would have avoided obvious steps toward leaving, such as purchasing large caravans of camels. And yet, because Nephi's family did leave Jerusalem with a large caravan, perhaps they already owned a large caravan and traveled often. We also know that Nephi was a capable hunter and archer.

From the outset, Nephi and his father don't appear to be overly religious. The first spiritual experience Nephi shares of his father occurs when his father was already an adult. Coincidentally, this is around the time when King Josiah rebuilt the temple and "rediscovered" the law of Moses. It seems fair to say that there is not an abundance of written scripture from this time. Additionally, Nephi's brothers, Laman and Lemuel, state that it is difficult to get scriptures.

Despite the lack of scriptures, Nephi knows Israelite history and draws inferences from it. When he was finally able to get scriptural records he was able to determine they only contained part of the prophecies of Jeremiah. Therefore, Nephi seems to be well-informed on current events.

Eventually, Nephi's father Lehi listens to prophets in Jerusalem and confirms their words in prayer. Lehi then joins the prophets in warning the citizens of Jerusalem to repent. Nephi is initially reluctant to believe his father, but his desire for knowledge leads him to pray. Nephi writes that the Lord softened his heart so he did believe the words spoken by his father. Later on, Nephi will reference "thoughts of the heart," and so it seems that Nephi ceded not only his desires but also his thoughts and beliefs to the Lord.

Now in retrospect it is obvious that Nephi should have left Jerusalem. However, at this time it was not clear the knowledge of Judah's wickedness was known throughout Jerusalem. Nephi's initial intent to remain in Jerusalem demonstrates perhaps he was not aware of the nation's vulnerable status. Later we also read that Laman and Lemuel allege those in Jerusalem were a righteous people and that Lehi was merely judgmental. Additionally, in the book of Ezekiel, Ezekiel is shown by God several nefarious deeds performed in Judah. At the time Ezekiel was not in Jerusalem, however, the fact that Ezekiel had to be shown these deeds suggests knowledge of them was not widespread and Ezekiel refers to what the "ancients of the house of Israel **do in the dark.**" Taken together, it would have made sense to Nephi to remain in Jerusalem. It appears he is reliant on prayerful confirmation to make what must have been a counter-intuitive decision.

At this point, Nephi is likely at least an adolescent. The confirmation he receives from the Lord drives Nephi to leave Jerusalem. As he is leaving, he acquires records that show him the true origin of his family tree. Nephi and his father are actually descendants of Joseph. This seems to indicate two things. First, Nephi's grandparents or great-grandparents were likely immigrants, as the children of

Joseph lived primarily in northern Israel. The Northern Kingdom of Israel had been destroyed about 100 years previously. Second, because ancestry is important in ancient Judaism, the fact that Nephi did not know about his family's origins implies perhaps it was not safe for Northern Israelites in Jerusalem. Only a short century earlier the Northern and Southern kingdoms were warring rivals.

There was also a powerful man in Jerusalem named Laban. Laban lived inside the famous walls of Jerusalem. We are told that he could command fifty people and that he could also slay fifty. He too was descendent of Joseph. Nephi's family was important enough in the community to get an audience with Laban. However, Laban tried to kill Nephi and his brothers over a property dispute. In my opinion, this implies that Nephi was still low enough in society that Laban thought he could be killed without much repercussion. After all, Nephi writes that he must go "up to Jerusalem." From the topography, we know he likely lived outside Jerusalem rather than in the city itself.

Nephi's Education

Nephi Knew Both Egyptian and Hebrew

As we mentioned, Nephi is portrayed as an aware and educated observer. Nephi's writings are some of the only autobiographical texts we have from that era, a sign of how precious recorded information can be. The Book of Tobit is another example of an autobiography of that age.

Nephi tells us he sought an audience with Laban to obtain records etched in brass. Nephi writes he had to get the brass plates to preserve the language for his children. So aside from language or secular knowledge, Nephi also says the brass plates contain the words spoken by the mouths of all the holy prophets. Because he needed to go so far out of his way to obtain them, I speculate that he did not have much written religious material available prior.

Noel Reynolds has demonstrated that scribes in this time were typically taught by their parents and had a separate vocation from their scribal duties. Additionally, most scribes of the time did have a repository of records (often referred to as a treasury). If this is true, Nephi and Lehi were likely administrative or legal scribes. Additionally, Demotic Egyptian (discussed later) of the time was used in administrative and legal settings. Regardless, one must question what type of schooling Nephi received. Notably all his writings are consistent with an Elohist tradition.

Now, Elohist is not a word Nephi would have used. The word *Elohist* was coined to describe a theory called "The Documentary Hypothesis," which identifies four specific literary styles in the Bible. These come from Jahwist (J), Elohist (E), Deuteronomist (D), and Priestly (P) sources.

Writing from the Elohist school of thought is associated with Northern Israel. These writers refer to God as Elohim early on in Israelite history. They accentuate Abraham's virtues and the Abrahamic covenant rather than the Davidic covenant. Elohist voices emphasize stories of Joseph. Additionally, Elohist passages paint Moses in a more positive light than those written in other traditions. We see those aspects in Nephi's writing and consistently throughout the whole Book of Mormon.

Details not mentioned above further evidence possible E effects on the Book of Mormon, either through the brass plates or through the family tradition in which Lehi was reared.

1. The Book of Mormon virtually ignores the Davidic covenant, a "J" element. David is mentioned but six times (two incidentally in quotations from Isaiah). Two instances involved strong condemnation of David.[34]

2. Instead, considerable attention is paid to the Abrahamic convenant and to the patriarchs. All twenty-nine references to Abraham are laudatory. Jacob is also so named, a positive E characteristic, whereas J uses "Israel" as his personal name.[35]

3. The Jews, particularly the inhabitants of Jerusalem, are branded as evil in the strongest terms.[36]

4. Emphasis is placed on Joseph being sold into Egypt, his saving Jacob's house, and the Lord's special covenant with Joseph which is not attested in the Old Testament.[37] The coat of Joseph is a topic specific to E on which the Book of Mormon adds data not found in the Jewish version (J).[38]

5. The name Jehovah, the preferred J title of deity, occurs only twice in the Book of Mormon (once in a quote from Isaiah 12—with one word changed—and once in the very last sentence in the volume). The name Lord is usually used for divinity in the Book of Mormon (almost 1400 times).[39]

6. Unmistakable El (E source) names do occur in the Book of Mormon, notably Most High God (Hebrew "El Elyon") and Almighty God (the Septuagint's term for "El Shaddai"),[40] the former six times and the latter eleven.

Indications of Elohist Tradition (Sorenson, 1997)

Another aspect of Jerusalem life upon which we may opine is based on a stark contrast between the writing of Lehi and Nephi. Nephi esteems his father's words highly and cites large sections of them. However, in those citations Lehi mentions Isaiah possibly once or twice. Whereas Nephi alludes to Isaiah several times in almost every chapter. Because Lehi is from a different generation, it seems reasonable that he may not have had the same access to Isaiah's words in his developmental years. Certainly, other conclusions are possible. However, this calls into question if Isaiah's words with its many prophecies and signs were widely circulated in Jerusalem at that time.

In 1 Nephi 20:6 the Lord asks Israel if it will not declare the signs that have been given it. I do not want to go down this tangent much, but indeed, there appears to possibly be a withholding of Isaiah's words. Not only does Lehi rarely use Isaiah, Nephi's very early conversations with his brothers contain few of the words of Isaiah and instead focus on the stories of Moses which are presumably more well known. It is only after Nephi obtains the brass plates that he cites Isaiah. Moving on we see this might give additional reason for Nephi to blame teachers or pastors for his forced departure. In 1 Nephi 21:1 he writes, "And again: hearken, O ye house of Israel, all ye that are broken off and are driven out because of the wickedness of the **pastors** of my people." Nephi's outspoken criticism of churches and church leaders will be one of the most defining characteristics of Nephi's writings. He appears to hold church leaders responsible for the "blood of the saints" in 2 Nephi 28:10.

This perspective helps us frame Laman and Lemuel in a slightly different light. Keep in mind that despite living in Jerusalem they probably did not have full access to much of the gospel early on. Much of what Laman and Lemuel were taught in the desert they were hearing for the first time.

Metalworking

Some have suggested that scribes were trained in metalworking because ultimately, they used metal plates (e.g., the foundation document found under King Darius' royal court in Persepolis or copper plates used by the Jews in Cochin, India). It makes sense that scribes might learn to make their writing material. So I don't have any problem with Nephi being a metalsmith as well as a scribe.

But what about steel? Steel is too hard as a writing material. Nephi appears to grade steel on occasion saying, "fine steel" in 1 Nephi 16:18 and "most precious" steel in 1 Nephi 4:9.

Another detail that suggests Nephi knows about steel is that Nephi tends to credit God when God teaches him. Yet Nephi never says God taught him metalsmithing. Rather, Nephi's question to God is "Where do I get ore to make tools?" and not, "How do I make tools?"

This brings us to something that was formerly controversial. Did the Jews have access to or knowledge about steel? Archeology has answered that for us. Steel swords have been found in Israel. But actually, we can learn more about Judean culture here. I suggest that steel and knowledge about steel were not very prevalent.

In a paper called "Early Evidence for Steelmaking in the Judaic Sources" Dan Levene describes a lot and I will only scratch the surface on this. He cites an ancient Hebrew script that reads Nebuchadnezzar sent 300 mules with axes made of "iron that prevails over iron." Keep in mind steel is iron with a little carbon infused (ideally no more than 2%). This will improve durability. Perhaps iron that prevails over iron is a reference to steel. At least that is what the author suggests.

Another reference to steel is in Jeremiah 15:2, which asks if a man can break iron and then it clarifies, "iron from the north." Is that a different type of iron? Levene suggests that is steel. Ezekiel 27:19 also may make mention of steel. It describes "bright iron" or "worked iron." Recall that carbon has to be infused or worked into the iron.

At face value it seems that steel exists, enough Jews know about it for prophets to allude to it in speeches. But, we also see that the Judeans of the period didn't seem to have a word for steel in their language. Perhaps they would if it were more commonplace. Also, when they talk about steel they mention it as coming from the north. The verse from Ezekiel, references "worked iron" from Tyre, north of Israel. Perhaps their listeners know about steel even if only as an import.

How does that apply to Nephi? Well, the ability to grade and work in steel is likely a very rare profession in Judah at that time. If Lehi has steel, it is no wonder Laban lusted after it. The expertise to make steel doesn't seem to exist in Jerusalem. Either Lehi is associated with a new guild of some sort in Jerusalem, or he has connections with Northern cities like Tyre and Nephi is learning there. Supporting that last point someone pointed out that Nephi's descendants name a river "Sidon" which is a city near Tyre in the north. Knowledge of steel would certainly explain Lehi's status as a sort of wealthy immigrant family in Judah.

Nephi refers to his treasures as "our gold...and our silver... and our precious things." Read as a list it seems "precious" refers to something besides gold or silver. The idea that steel is more precious than gold is also alluded to, in the description of Laban's sword as well. It is the steel that is described as most precious, not the gold. So, perhaps Lehi has pieces of steel and that is what Laban lusts over.

A final piece to add to the mix seems to be weapons production. Nephi seems very competent at weapon usage. He notes the need to make new arrows after making a different bow. Indeed, bows of different weights use different arrows for optimum effectiveness. Nephi also records producing swords.

This is not just academic. I care about this because it reframes how we see Nephi and statements he made. Nephi had to reinvent himself and become a spiritual leader himself. That is part of the journey that we miss and may not appreciate. We can believe Nephi when he says his heart had to be softened to leave Jerusalem. Perhaps he too thought it could not fall. He would likely have known of the city's possibly cutting-edge weapons technology at the time. At some time or another all the house of Israel tends to trust in military might to save them (the Lord shows them it won't).

We can also read Nephi's text and consider there is a grudge against the Jewish elders. As mentioned, he explicitly blames them for the destruction of Jerusalem (1 Nephi 21:1). In that verse he seems to otherize religious leaders. His rhetoric about churches in the last days is some of the most negative found in the Book of Mormon. Perhaps there is something personal in Nephi's denouncement of church leaders. After all, Nephi thrived in his expertise for the benefit of Jerusalem; he expected other professionals to do the same.

What is Important to Nephi? Language

The Anthon Transcript or "Caractors Document" Via the Community of Christ

As Nephi leaves Jerusalem, he states that he needs the brass plates to "preserve...the language of our fathers. And the words which have been spoken by the mouth of all the holy prophets."

That may sound peculiar. Nephi is leaving all civilization, and he wants to bring a book to preserve language. In all the disaster movies I have seen, I don't think I have ever seen a fleeing person grab a dictionary or a grammar book as they leave home. Why did this occur to Nephi?

Words are vitally important to our civilization. Knowledge is contained within our language. For example, consider these few words from a chemistry glossary:

> Adsorption
> Aerobic
> Alkaline
> Atomic Weight
> Buffer
> Catalyst
> Condensate
> Conductivity
> Decant
> Effluent
> Emulsion

If all you know is the definition of these words, you have a grasp of those chemistry principles. If you can explain and talk about these words, you're on your way to a fairly decent knowledge of chemistry.

Language is important to Nephi because it embodies knowledge. Different languages do more than affix different words to the same concepts. Each language embodies different concepts; it is not a stretch to say that there is knowledge to be found in words and foreign languages. Aside from the Egyptian words, each of the 800 or so hieroglyphs used in ancient Egypt has its own historical background. A language contains a wealth of knowledge.

In Mosiah 1:4, we learn that the brass plates sought by Nephi are inscribed with Egyptian characters. Therefore, it appears Nephi has a copy of many of Isaiah's words, the writings of Jeremiah, and the book of Moses[1] in Egyptian. There is no consensus among Latter-day Saint scholars if these Egyptian characters represented Egyptian or Hebrew words. There is a precedence of non-Egyptian languages being transliterated in Egyptian (i.e., Papyrus Amherst 63).

Regardless, given the family's status and position it appears likely Laman and Lemuel can read and write Hebrew. We will discuss that shortly. However, it seems Nephi's brothers cannot read Egyptian. On one occasion, they ask Nephi, "What meaneth these things which *ye have read?*" and another time Nephi writes, "I did read many things to them … *that they might know*" what was written on the plates of brass. The leap from writing Hebrew with about 20 letters to Egyptian with hundreds of symbols is vast.

---

[1] The original translation of the Book of Mormon reads that the brass plates contained the "book of Moses" and not "the five books of Moses," as modern translations render that phrase.

The Egyptian Writing Nephi Used

Hieroglyphic	Hieroglyphic Book Hand	Hieratic			Demotic
					(:˒ᵓ𝔐)
2700-2600 B.C.	ca. 1500 B.C.	ca. 1500 B.C.	ca. 1900 B.C.	ca. 200 B.C.	400-100 B.C.

Forms of Egyptian Writing (Steindorff)

Beautiful, puzzling, and mysterious hieroglyphics have confounded researchers for centuries. These hieroglyphs have both logographic and syllabic meanings. That is, some symbols signify an entire word and others only a sound. Because of the vast number of characters, Egyptian writing is more concise than our style of alphabetic writing, but one can imagine how overwhelming it could be to learn.

In her book, *Ancient Egyptian Literature*, Miriam Lichtheim writes that around 700 BCE a new Egyptian writing system arose, called Demotic. Demotic symbols often correlate to a previously existing hieroglyph. Altogether then there are at least four versions of most symbols. Hieroglyphic writing is used for public purposes, such as inscriptions on monuments. There was also Hieroglyphic book hand that allowed for quicker writing. There was a form of characters called Hieratic as well. Hieratic writing is used for religious documents. The majority of text in versions of the *Book of the Dead* is written in Hieratic. The last form of writing, Demotic, draws its name from the Greek word for "common." In its lowercase form, "demotic" still refers to commonly used language. While Demotic became at one point the more common form of Egyptian writing, it was certainly not called Demotic at the time. Lichtheim describes Demotic as hieratic cursive and the first Demotic writings were typically used for legal agreements and receipts.

The brass plates may have been written in Demotic or hieratic Egyptian. Prophets such as Zenock and Zenos, whose writings were also on the brass plates, were likely from the Northern Kingdom of Israel. They were also from the tribe of Joseph (3 Nephi 10:16). Because the Northern Kingdom was destroyed before 700 BCE, the writings on the brass plates are probably older. Unless Northern Israel pioneered Demotic writing, it seems based on the age of the writings that the brass plates were written in hieratic.

However, it appears Nephi wrote in the hieratic cursive which we call Demotic today. This is based on a surviving copy of the characters Joseph Smith allowed to be copied from Nephi's plates. A surviving document previously called the "Anthon Transcript" is a copy of some characters from the Nephite gold plates. Roughly a dozen people saw and handled the gold plates. Handwriting analysis suggests the characters on the document were copied by John Whitmer. These characters don't look like any language to me, but when placed side by side with demotic glyphs they reveal numerous similarities.

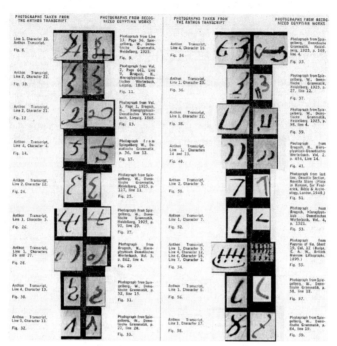

Altogether, given the similarities with Demotic and these characters as well as the age of the brass plates, **it seems that Nephi knows both hieratic and hieratic cursive,** or what we call Demotic today.

In passing, Nephi states that his spoken word was much more powerful than his writing. So it seems there are some aspects of Nephi's message that we are missing.

Nephi's Name; More Egyptian Influence?

Language	Root/source	Meaning
Hebrew	2 Maccabees 1:36	cleansing agent
Egyptian	nfr	good
Egyptian	nfy and npw	captain
North-Western Semitic	nph	to breath/ to blow
Coptic	neef	to breath/ to blow
West Semitic	nph	to banish
Arabic	nafaiy	exile
Ugaritic	npy	to drive away, expel

Possible Meanings of "Nephi"

The influence of Egypt is not limited to Nephi's writing. It turns out that the consonants in Nephi's name were common in multiple languages. In Hebrew, Egyptian and Arabic, "nephi" can mean "cleansing", "captain," or "exile" respectively. In my opinion, Nephi's name is best understood to mean "captain." In Nephi's writings, we read that Laman and Lemuel should follow the "captain." The captain is needed to steer the boat, and most convincingly, Jacob states that the Nephites intend to call their leaders First Nephi, Second Nephi, Third Nephi, and so forth. According to our current knowledge, this would suggest additional Egyptian influence on Nephi's family. Certainly, Nephi can mean "good," or "a cleansing agent" instead. Alternatively, the terms "cleansing" and "captain" might not have been culturally exclusive at that time. Strangely, as Nephi is the embodiment of Israel being exiled from Jerusalem, the Arabic definition of "exile" seems very fitting as well.

Nephi and Paleo-Hebrew

Arad Ostraca Circa 600 BCE (Faigenbaum-Golovin, 2016)

Let's turn our attention to Hebrew for a moment. After all, Mormon states there would be no error in the record if its authors had had room to write in Hebrew.

The block-style Hebrew letters we are familiar with were adopted in Babylon by the Jews during their exile there. In the modern-day we would label the Hebrew style used by Nephi as "Paleo-Hebrew."

Literacy rates for Hebrew in ancient Israel have been estimated as high as 20%, which would have made it a very literate society. This estimate is based on handwriting analysis of fragments found in Tel Arad. There, a small fort that would only have held about 20 soldiers contains examples written with different handwriting. Additionally, many of the writings found at Tel Arad are instructions to lower-level military officials, reinforcing the notion that a good portion of the populace was literate. These shards date to Nephi's time, and this is, therefore, the form of Hebrew he most likely used.

Language: Conclusion

As part of any literary analysis, it is key to ask what is valued. What is valued both by society and what is valued by the individual people in it? Because what one chooses to value is a matter of individual choice, one of the most basic ways we can understand a person's mindset and circumstances is to understand what is valued. In this way, we understand people and ourselves better. It is, therefore, crucial to re-emphasize the importance that Nephi gives to both knowledge and language. Remember, this is the person who upon fleeing Jerusalem states they need to preserve both the language and the law of Moses. Nephi then brings the brass plates containing a generous written record. I wonder what I would take if I had to similarly leave my homeland.

Nephi on Growth

Nephi's personal development is evident over the course of his two books. Nephi writes that he intends to demonstrate to the reader that God makes his people strong to the point of deliverance and to me it appears Nephi does this by demonstrating his own growth.

1) He starts young, intent on remaining in his homeland of Jerusalem.

2) Later, he chooses to follow his father and flee the city.

3) He then completes several assignments from God that are relayed by his father, such as getting the brass plates.

4) Then he begins to receive personal instructions directly from the Lord.

5) Following the Lord's instructions, he becomes a role model and leader to his older brothers.

6) He forges tools and weapons in the middle of the desert with minimal materials.

7) Nephi then constructs ocean-worthy seacraft.

8) He later becomes a writer, a teacher, a founder of cities, and a builder of temples, and is considered a king by some (Jacob 1:11).

9) Finally, he is a person who knowingly (2 Nephi 25:21) assists with the preservation and gathering of Israel "that the promise made to Joseph may be fulfilled that his seed should never perish."

One reason Nephi shares his life is that he doesn't believe that he is special. He writes his life in a way to show that God blesses him and would likewise do so for **anyone else** who follows similar steps. Nephi shares his life to show "that the tender mercies of the Lord are over all those whom he hath chosen, because of their faith**, to make them mighty even unto the power of deliverance**."

From that preceding list, an undaunting task is to build an ocean-worthy seacraft. How did Nephi do that? His brothers confirm that shipbuilding was not in Nephi's ability. How did Nephi obtain such knowledge? Can we access the same sources?

Nephi states that he "did go into the mount oft, and...did pray oft unto the Lord; wherefore the Lord showed unto me great things." Nephi does associate the presence of God with knowledge as we will later see.

However, when Nephi writes about when he is given knowledge he writes that the Lord "hath given me knowledge by visions in the night-time." Furthermore, he writes that his "heart pondereth continually upon the things which [he] has seen and heard." Therefore, we can surmise that aside from living uprightly, Nephi *thought* with a great deal of effort on things. The word he used translates as "ponder" which shares derivation with the word "pound." Nephi thinks on his dilemmas as if there is a weight on his head. This is echoed by a brother of Nephi who writes it is because of faith and "great anxiety" they get similar revelations (Jacob 1:5).

Aside from Nephi, inventors and musicians have also stated many of their ideas came to them in a dream. This was of course during times these individuals were intensely studying. Examples include Paul McCartney's song 'Yesterday,' and the periodic table by Dimitri Mendeleev. Albert Einstein himself states that as a teenager he dreamt about the principles of relativity.

I want to emphasize the implications here. Firstly, even in this world, to some degree we are all within the presence of God therefore we all have access to some inspiration. Secondly, it appears that aside from living an upright life we must continually think on the dilemmas to which we need solutions.

Altogether, it seems this is the method Nephi demonstrates for solving problems such as building a reliable boat without prior experience. He prays, goes to the mountain often, ponders continuously and is available at night.

Dichotomy in the World Where Nephi Grew Up

To get a better sense of Nephi as a person, we need to consider the world he grew up in as well. Nephi's decision to leave Jerusalem was monumentally important. What do we know of Nephi's Jerusalem, and how did it shape his character?

Nephi portrays Jerusalem as a land of prosperity, blessings, and worldwide influence. Who wouldn't have wanted to live there? Jerusalem likely had all the complexities of a major hub that had been established for hundreds of years. More than 300 years before Nephi lived, King Solomon ruled in Jerusalem at the height of its recorded power. Nephi surely would have been aware of Jerusalem's status and glory.

Nephi could still view Solomon's temple. In Chronicles, we learn that the sacred temple wall was built with more than "3,000 talents of gold, of the gold of Ophir." A talent in ancient Israel was a measure of weight corresponding to about 75 pounds. Altogether, 3,000 talents would have been roughly 250,000 pounds of gold. Today, that amount of gold would be worth about $5.5 billion USD.

So, the kingdom of Israel was doing well. But riches alone do not make a healthy society or a powerful kingdom. At Jerusalem's height, great wisdom was given to King Solomon. When the Queen of Sheba traveled to Jerusalem, she realized that the rumors of its grandeur did not do the city justice. She admitted, "behold the half was not told me: thy wisdom and prosperity exceedeth the fame which I heard (1 Kings 10)."

300 years later, Nephi saw the Temple of Solomon restored by King Josiah. He was surrounded by reminders of a bygone golden age. It is hard to know how much of Solomon's Jerusalem was intact in that time.

But little was wasted on Nephi. Nephi quotes Isaiah as saying that God would "**make a man more precious than fine gold; even a man than the golden wedge of Ophir** (2 Nephi 23:22)." We are unsure how much treasure came from Ophir, and it is likely that only a small part was used to build Solomon's temple. Because at least 3,000 talents were used for the wall alone the total treasure is larger. Nephi then is saying in essence that **God intends to make people worth over \$5 billion**—an almost unthinkable amount then and now. That is just a hint as to how much God values us.

So Nephi knows the true worth and potential of people. He knows the work of the Lord is to refine and edify each one of us. Nephi could not walk through Jerusalem without being reminded of its history. He knew that when people obey God, good things happen. Nephi reminds his brothers of this. When men follow God, even slaves can evade armies and chariots (1 Nephi 4:2).

Robert T. Barrett, **Moses Parting the Red Sea.** © 1983 *Intellectual Reserve, Inc.*

However, Nephi also comes to learn that those in Jerusalem did "works of darkness." The works occurring in Jerusalem included slavery and human sacrifice, so there is a stark contrast between the Jerusalem Nephi sees and the one he hears about. On one hand, he lives near the Holy City. The city that should be a host of God's kingdom, where God's work is performed, and man edified. On the other hand, he sees in front of him humans who are no more than slaves, and children who are deemed worthy only of sacrifice to some minor deity. At times, these human sacrifices were led by the very King of Judah. King Ahaz "burnt his children in the fire, after the abominations of the heathen whom the Lord had cast out before the children of Israel (2 Chronicles 28:3)."

Despite witnessing these dreadful crimes against humankind, Nephi never stops talking and writing about Jerusalem's restoration, even 40 years after leaving the city. Nephi lived in a world of the highest highs and the lowest lows. Both greatness and destruction are linked to righteousness or its absence.

THE
NEW YORKER

LETTER FROM ISRAEL   JUNE 29, 2020 ISSUE

IN SEARCH OF KING DAVID'S LOST EMPIRE

The Biblical ruler's story has been told for millennia. Archeologists are still fighting over whether it's true.

By Ruth Margalit

Margalit, The New Yorker, 2020

To be clear, some skeptics argue whether Judah and Israel ever existed. One might wonder how little we know about details of their everyday lives if we aren't even sure they exist. Luckily, several archeological finds support the existence of a thriving empire centered in Jerusalem near 1,000 BCE.

Archaeologists began investigating the copper mines south of Jerusalem. More than 10,000 mines, camps, and smelting sites have been found in the region. King Solomon's Mines, it appears, are not a myth but a fact of history.

PLOS ONE

🔓 OPEN ACCESS   🖊 PEER-REVIEWED

RESEARCH ARTICLE

Early evidence of royal purple dyed textile from Timna Valley (Israel)

Naama Sukenik 🌐 📧, David Iluz, Zohar Amar, Alexander Varvak, Orit Shamir, Erez Ben-Yosef 🌐 📧

Published: January 28, 2021 • https://doi.org/10.1371/journal.pone.0245897

Sukenik, 2021

While exploring mines in Timna Valley, archaeologists discovered fragments of purple fabrics. Chromatography confirmed a rare purple molecule that is exclusively found in specific mollusks. Carbon dating places this cloth and surrounding organic matter in the 10th century BCE. We tend associate purple with wealth and power—in many cultures, purple was a color that only the rich could wear, partly because purple dyes were rare and expensive. This was the case in Jerusalem. Each mollusk produced only nine-tenths of a gram of purple dye: it took roughly 50,000 mollusks to dye a single sleeve. The presence of purple supports the idea that the Jerusalem of

Solomon's time supported a stable economic infrastructure and a significant upper class.

But what does Timna Valley look like now? There is hardly a trace of anything there. I can hardly blame skeptics for wondering if a thriving society ever took hold in the region.

Timna Valley

After all, Jeremiah wrote, "Thus saith the Lord...I will make thee a wilderness (Jeremiah 22:6)." Jeremiah went on to write, "And many nations shall pass by...and say every man to his neighbor, wherefore hath the Lord done thus? ...Then they shall answer, 'Because they have forsaken the covenant of the Lord.'"

Nephi was not in Jerusalem at the time of its destruction. However, he saw its destruction in a vision, as well as its eventual millennial glory. Hence, Nephi is aware that both success and failure are linked to either righteousness or its absence.

Perhaps part of the hype about the Book of Mormon is that in Nephi's writings church members see a pathway to avoid destruction or subjugation and a pattern for achieving strength, knowledge, and independence.

Chapter 2

Nephi's Writing

Determining the Audience

Now that we have established the setting in which Nephi lived, we can take a look at the surviving examples of his writing. Like any writer, Nephi had an audience in mind. Knowing a bit about his audience can help us understand what Nephi meant to say in his writing, and why he chose to write as he did.

While Nephi initially states, "the Lord hath commanded me to make these plates for a wise purpose in him, which purpose I know not (1 Nephi 9:5)," he later appears to develop at least a partial sense of his audience, though he stops short of any sort of assurance that his people will read what he writes. Yet, the plates are for the "instruction of [his] people who should possess the land, and also for other wise purposes which purposes are known unto the Lord (1 Nephi 19:3)." However, Nephi also considered others reading his text near the end of his writing. He doesn't appear to address to the same audience. He writes in 2 Nephi 33, "I, Nephi, cannot write all the things which were taught among my people." He then writes, "my beloved brethren, all those who are of the house of Israel, and all ye ends of the earth." Altogether, it seems safe to say that Nephi tends to anticipate a broad audience, extending beyond his people.

First and Second Nephi

Nephi himself wrote approximately 100 pages, which are split into two books called 1 and 2 Nephi. 3 and 4 Nephi were written later and are about other people. This is a modern arrangement. Looking at the printer's manuscript for the Book of Mormon, it seems the terms "first" and "second" were added after translation. To Nephi, these books are not 1 Nephi and 2 Nephi as we tend to cite them. Instead, they are books of Nephi.

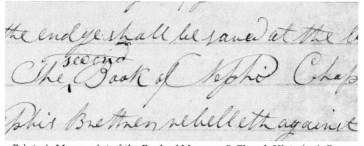

Printer's Manuscript of the Book of Mormon © Church Historian's Press

The record was written 30-40 years after the events it describes. This gap allowed Nephi to reflect thoughtfully on what he had to say and to record his observations in a way that had already stood the test of time.

Nephi's writings are not meant to be a comprehensive history of his times. He already had an extensive record of his people. He titles 1 Nephi "Book of Nephi: his Reign and Ministry." Today we might classify 1 Nephi as a memoir or autobiography. The opening of 1 Nephi is most similar with the Book of Tobit which is autobiographical and from the same period. The Lord told him specifically to write a record of his ministry. It appears that is what he did in 1 Nephi.

Second Nephi is much more puzzling. It references the last chapter of 1 Nephi in which he taught his brothers. Nephi writes, "after, I, Nephi had made an end of teaching my brethren." So 2 Nephi appears attached to 1 Nephi but all other markings indicate the book is a **legal document.** Perhaps the reason for a book division is to signal this is not a continuation of an autobiography.

In the following I discuss legal culture of Judah and ancient Mesopotamia. It is heavily annotated as this section is pending publication in an edition of the *Interpreter*. If you would like to skip this section continue on page 109 "Nephi's Optimism."

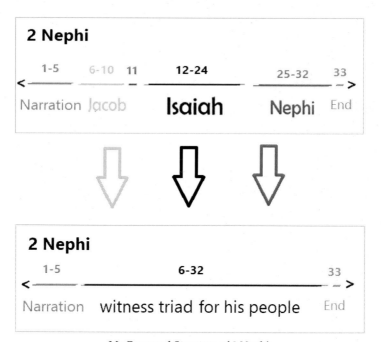

My Proposed Structure of 2 Nephi

Second Nephi as a Legal Text[2]

Considering conventions of the ancient Near East, 2 Nephi can be understood as a legal document or legal archive. Factors supporting this view include: 1) Nephi's allusions to sealing the record and to a bar of judgment, 2) discussion of the law of witnesses and reference to Isaiah and Jacob as witnesses, 3) components and formatting consistent with Neo-Babylonian depositions and plaintiff statements, 4) uncharacteristically formal and conservative (high-fidelity) citations of Isaiah, and 5)

---

[2] This section is reproduced. Currently it is in production through the *Interpreter* journal.

rhetoric and vocabulary consistent with the Judean legal genre.

Nephi's inclusion of Jacob's and Isaiah's words as a witness and his references to judicial procedure can be readily understood. Further, the structure of 2 Nephi, consistent with legal conventions of the time, can be viewed as collated texts that contain a covenant framing the Nephite's situation (2 Nephi 1-4), a reaction (2 Nephi 4-5), three supporting witness statements (2 Nephi 6-10, 12-24, 25-28), and finally a plaintiff statement (2 Nephi 33). Recognizing the legal implications of 2 Nephi can help us appreciate Nephi's agenda as author and editor of his text, as well as the meaning of his document in our day.

Introduction and Literature Review

The Book of Mormon contains an abridgment of many records from the people of Nephi. Within the Book of Mormon, there are also two unabridged books written by Nephi. These books were written in the sixth century BCE, approximately one thousand years before the main corpus of the Book of Mormon. Cultural changes will invariably occur over time and some changes may have been deliberate (2 Nephi 25:2). Consideration of contemporary ancient Near Eastern customs may be critical in understanding Nephi's text.

The second book of Nephi has confounded readers for more than 100 years. Highlighting its importance, Elder Jeffrey R Holland stated, "standing like sentinels at the gate of the [Book of Mormon]," the writings in 2 Nephi "admit us into the scriptural presence of the Lord."[3] Some readers, however, may feel 2 Nephi is a "compilation of instructive but unrelated incidents, doctrines, and prophecies."[4] Perhaps because the book of 2 Nephi remains enigmatic, its structure has been the subject of sustained inquiry over many years.[5] While there are many perspectives, few of them are mutually exclusive. Some secular scholars have opined that 2 Nephi is a collection of contextless excerpts and reflections[6] or commentary interwoven with scripture.[7] Brant Gardner writes that Nephi starts to write a narrative, but later his intent changes, and he includes a sermon.[8] Frederick Axelgard

---

[3] Jeffrey R. Holland, *Christ and the New Covenant: The Messianic Message of the Book of Mormon* (Salt Lake City, UT: Deseret Book, 1997), 34–36.

[4] Frederick Axelgard, "1 and 2 Nephi: An Inspiring Whole," *BYU Studies Quarterly* 26, no. 4 (Oct. 1986): 53–65, https://scholarsarchive.byu.edu/cgi/viewcontent.cgi?article=2476&context=byusq.

[5] Monte S. Nyman and Charles D. Tate Jr., *The Book of Mormon: Second Nephi, the Doctrinal Structure*, Book of Mormon Symposium Series (Provo, UT: Religious Studies Center, Brigham Young University, 1989).

[6] Hardy writes 2 Nephi contains "undated, contextless excerpts, along with reflections."; see Grant Hardy, *Understanding the Book of Mormon: A Reader's Guide* (Oxford: Oxford University Press, 2010), https://doi.org/10.1093/acprof:oso/9780199731701.001.0001.

[7] Benjamin L. McGuire, "Nephi: A Postmodernist Reading," *Interpreter: A Journal of Mormon Scripture* 14 (2014): 49-78, https://journal.interpreterfoundation.org/nephi-a-postmodernist-reading/

[8] Gardner writes that Nephi was planning on 2 Nephi to be a narrative (based on the header for 2 Nephi). "That was Nephi's plan. His plan was short-lived." He writes that 2 Nephi 4 was a "emotional and poetic response to his father's passing, one spontaneous rather than planned." Nephi resumed the narrative in 2 Nephi 5 then pauses without finishing it (the chapter doesn't end with "Amen" which Gardner

argues for a holistic interpretation of both books written by Nephi. He notes the spiritual themes in 2 Nephi parallel the historical themes in 1 Nephi; they have similar themes presented in the same order.[9] Joseph Spencer places Isaiah's encounter with God (2 Nephi 16) as the central part of 2 Nephi. He shows that Nephi uses Isaiah's encounter with God as a paradigm for how God interacts with all His children.[10] Spencer suggests Nephi has much of 2 Nephi in mind when he refers to "more sacred things (1 Nephi 19:5)." Spencer has also reasonably suggested modern readers overlook a major division within 2 Nephi, which should be placed prior to 2 Nephi 6:1.[11] Noel

---

shows is an idiosyncrasy of Nephi's). When Nephi returns to the record, "he had intended to speak of wars and contentions. … but decided to change the way he had been writing. Rather than narrate a story of contentions, he entered a sermon from Jacob that was designed and delivered to ease the contentions." Brant Gardner, "Labor Diligently to Write: The Ancient Making of a Modern Scripture Chapters 6 – 8," *Interpreter: A Journal of Latter-day Saint Faith and Scholarship* 35 (2020): 107-166, https://archive.bookofmormoncentral.org/content/labor-diligently-write-ancient-making-modern-scripture-chapters-6-8. Gardner's view is also similar to Given's. He states 2 Nephi provides a "defining charter for this new community." Brant Gardner, *Analytical and contextual commentary on the Book of Mormon: Second Nephi - Jacob* (Salt Lake City: Greg Kofford Books, 2007), 15

[9] Axelgard, "1 And 2 Nephi."

[10] Spencer writes 2 Nephi 16 is the "structurally privileged" Isaiah 6-12 is, we've said, Second Nephi's heart of hearts. But now let's note that there's another structural feature of Nephi's record that privileges Isaiah 6 still further." Joseph M. Spencer, *The Vision of All: Twenty-five Lectures on Isaiah in Nephi's Record* (Salt Lake City: Greg Kofford Books, 2016), 170.

[11] Spencer writes, "Nephi's record divides into two major parts: (1) the twenty-seven chapters stretching from 1 Nephi 1 to 2 Nephi 5, leading up to the account of the physical production of the small plates; and (2)

Reynolds' states this, "challenge[s] the book divisions left to us by the original author." Reynolds demonstrates there is an overarching symmetrical (chiastic) structure centered on 2 Nephi 11. Thereby, 2 Nephi presents itself foremost as a witness of Christ, which is the theme of 2 Nephi 11.[12] Reynolds continues by saying 2 Nephi "elevates the traditional meaning of the Abrahamic/Lehitic promises ... into a focus on... Christ."[13] Terryl Given's comments are similar; he shows that 2 Nephi establishes a broader Nephite identity. Givens does this by comparing the Nephite's history with that of the Jews exiled in Babylon. Givens notes the Babylonian exile was met with a counter-reaction that solidified Jewish thought, text and language. He points out the Babylonian exile ultimately led to the production and adoption of the Torah. Similarly, the Nephites, unnerved by the fall of Jerusalem, the center of Jewish worship, needed to forge a new identity. Second Nephi reassures there is a *new* land of promise.[14]

---

the twenty-eight chapters stretching from 2 Nephi 6 to 2 Nephi 33, following the account of the physical production of the small plates." Joseph M. Spencer, *An Other Testament: On Typology* (Salem, OR: Salt Press, 2012), 34-35.

[12] Noel Reynolds, "On Doubting Nephi's Break Between 1 and 2 Nephi: A Critique of Joseph Spencer's 'An Other Testament: On Typology,'" BYU Faculty Publications, 2017, https://scholarsarchive.byu.edu/facpub/1806.

[13] Noel B. Reynolds, "Chiastic Structuring of Large Texts: 2 Nephi as a Case Study," in Jack Welch and Donald Parry, eds., *Chiasmus: The State of the Art* (BYU Studies & Book of Mormon Central, 2020), 190, https://byustudies.byu.edu/article/chiastic-structuring-of-large-texts-2-nephi-as-a-case-study/.

[14] Terryl Givens, *2nd Nephi: A Brief Theological Introduction* (Provo, UT: The Neal A Maxwell Institute for Religious Scholarship, 2019), 4-6.

Taylor Halverson points out 2 Nephi contains covenants and is therefore law for the Nephites. He writes 2 Nephi contains "Lehi's last will and covenantal speech."[15] John Welch has also demonstrated the initial portion of 2 Nephi is the ancient equivalent of Lehi's will and testament. Lehi's words establish Nephi as a leader, adopt Zoram, and more.[16] According to Welch this text functions as a "legal and constitutional basis for several future centuries of Nephite thought and life." He notes these initial chapters contain similar components as legal ancient Near Eastern texts. Jan Martin suggests Jerusalem was so fundamental and crucial in First Temple period religion and culture that it may have been the announcement of the destruction of Jerusalem that prompted the division of 1 and 2 Nephi.[17] She adds to this by demonstrating the initial five chapters of 2 Nephi are a highly structured suzerain covenant consistent with ancient Near Eastern tradition. Martin identifies sections within 2 Nephi containing a preamble, historical prologue, stipulations, blessings and cursings, and instructions for preserving and remembering the

---

[15] Book of Mormon, see Taylor Halverson, *The Covenant Path in the Bible and the Book of Mormon* (Springville, UT: Line of Sight Publishing, 2020), 228

[16] John W. Welch, "Lehi's Last Will and Testament: A Legal Approach," in *The Book of Mormon: Second Nephi, the Doctrinal Structure*, ed. Monte S. Nyman and Charles D. Tate Jr. (Provo, UT: Religious Studies Center, Brigham Young University, 1989), 61–82, https://rsc.byu.edu/book-mormon-second-nephi-doctrinal-structure/lehis-last-will-testament-legal-approach.

[17] Jan Martin "The Prophet Nephi and the Covenantal Nature of Cut-off, Cursed, Skin of Blackness, and Loathsome," in *They Shall Grow Together: The Bible in the Book of Mormon*, ed. Charles Swift and Nicholas Frederick (Provo, UT: Religious Studies Center, 2022), 107–141.

covenant. However, a final component of suzerain treaties that appears absent on initial evaluation is a list or mention of witnesses. Juxtaposing the covenantal documents of Deuteronomy and 2 Nephi, Martin states,

> Moses specified that the "heavens" and the "earth" were witnesses (Deuteronomy 32:1), and he directed that large, inscribed stones be set up on the banks of the river Jordan as witnesses to Israel's covenant renewal (see Deuteronomy 27:1-3). If Lehi did something similar with objects, Nephi did not record it on the small plates.[18]

Martin continues, "Lehi's descendants, who were all present at the covenant-renewal ceremony, could easily have served as the witnesses to the covenant."

Herein, I agree with Givens and Halverson. The book of 2 Nephi is tantamount to a manifesto that forms the ethos and law of the Nephite nation. I differ from Welch as I hold more than the first section of 2 Nephi can be understood as a legal text. I agree with Spencer that a significant division could be made between 2 Nephi chapters 5 and 6. Reynold's chiastic model strengthens my position; he writes 2 Nephi 11 is the center-most part of 2 Nephi. It is in this section that Nephi writes "by the words of three, God ... will establish [His] word. Nevertheless, God sendeth more *witnesses*" (vs. 3). It may seem straightforward that 2 Nephi contains witness statements, but this paper demonstrates Nephi uses conventions seen in ancient legal proceedings to present these witness statements. Therefore in contrast to Martin, I hold there *is* an explicit identification of witnesses within 2 Nephi. Yet,

---

[18] Martin, *"The Prophet Nephi,"* 113

Martin's insights solidify our anticipation that witnesses should be provided in the record following Lehi's words.

The Concept of Objects as a Witness in Ancient Mesopotamia

In modern convention we may use the word "witness" to refer to people that can attest to specific events. But as Martin points out, objects, even stones, could stand as a witness. It is well understood that an object could function as a witness in the ancient Near East. Most legal transactions were presumably oral, but objects and persons qualified as witnesses. Documents,[19] carcasses, garments, or oaths could be used as a witness.[20] This knowledge helps inform our reading of texts originating in that place and time. For example, in the narrative of Joseph, Potiphar's wife used Joseph's garment to support her accusations against him. The sons of Israel also presented Joseph's torn garment as proof of his demise. These stories are not depicted as legal procedures, but the included objects lead us to conjecture how a public official would view the events.

Material Culture of Documents

To the ancient Israelites, the tablets containing the Ten Commandments are more than written admonitions. The tablets themselves are a proof of the covenant with God (Exodus 31:18). Beyond functioning as a witness, the material culture also held that inscriptions were

---

[19] Bruce Wells, *The Law of Testimony in the Pentateuchal Codes* (Wiesbaden, Germany: Harrassowitz, 2004), 127

[20] Raymond Westbrook and Bruce Wells, *Everyday Law in Biblical Israel: An Introduction* (London: Westminster John Knox Press, 2009), 42.

essentially a character in their own right. Objects may witness, but they also act and can secure or guarantee future outcomes.[21] A quintessential example of this material culture is depicted by foundation documents. For approximately three thousand years cultures in Mesopotamia constructed buildings over stone boxes containing documents (often metal). By placing written texts underneath notable buildings or within foundations a king effectively says "every aspect of human civilized culture- the civilizing tendency itself, which gives birth to the temple, the palace, the city-state, his entire kingdom, and even to his own powers-is built upon the written

---

[21] Cited for additional cultural context: "This conception of writing as material witness is demonstrated in Jeremiah 32 where the prophet buys a field during the siege of Jerusalem… The double-form of the deed — a sealed and an open copy are mentioned (Jer 32:11, 14)— itself demonstrates the double-signification of writing: the open copy allows public review and repeated proclamation, even if, or after, the witnesses to the transfer event are not themselves available; meanwhile, the sealed copy exists as a persistent thing which witnesses to the originating and ongoing event. In this way, the written deed recollects the written law, which seems also to have existed in double-form: the tablets inscribed by God sealed within the Ark, a persistent material witness to covenant, and the copy inscribed by Moses placed beside the Ark as witness, allowing for ongoing publication and re-proclamation… Further, Jeremiah 32 does not merely recount the legal niceties of property transfer in ancient Judah, but continues to stress the power of inscription's persistence, as Jeremiah charges the scribe Baruch with the LORD's own command to take both deeds, the sealed and the open, "and put them in an earthenware jar, in order that they may last for a long time" (Jer 32:14)." See Katherine E. Brown, "Silent Idol, Speaking Text: Prophetic Writing as Material Mediation of Divine Presence" (Ph.D. Dissertation, Washington, D.C., The Catholic University of America, 2018), 102-106, https://cuislandora.wrlc.org/islandora/object/cuislandora%3A213600/d atastream/PDF/view.

document."[22] In his paper "An Everlasting Witness: Ancient Writings on Metal," Reynolds demonstrates just as in the Near East, the Nephites also viewed writing as a witness. He writes that the Nephites knew "metal plates would play a major role in God's final work." That vision resulted in creating, transmitting and maintaining written witnesses.[23] Aspects of 2 Nephi allow it to be viewed as a witness in its time for *multiple* reasons. The book of 2 Nephi contains unique cultural and legal components contemporary readers would clearly understand.

Throughout the ancient Near East, documents were produced by professional scribes whose training and standing stood as guarantees of their documents' validity. Parties to legal actions in Nephi's time need not have signed legal documents to confirm their validity.[24] The

---

[22] H. Curtis Wright, "Ancient Burials of Metal Documents in Stone Boxes," in *By Study and Also By Faith, Volume 2* edited by John M. Lundquist and Stephen D. Ricks (Provo, UT/Salt Lake City, Utah: Foundation for Ancient Research and Mormon Studies/Deseret Book, 1990), 302. As a contemporary example, one document found at under the Apadana at Persepolis was inscribed in gold and read, "Darius the Great King, King of Kings, King of countries, son of Hystaspes, an Achacmenian. Saith Darius the King: this is the kingdom which I hold, from the Scythians who are beyond Sogdiana, thence unto Ethiopia; from Sind, thence unto Sardis which Ahuramazda the greatest of gods bestowed upon me. May Ahuramazda protect me and my royal house." Margaret Cool Root, 'The Persian Archer at Persepolis: Aspects of Chronology, Style, and Symbolism,' Revue des études anciennes 91 (1989) 33-50.

[23] See Noel B. Reynolds, "An Everlasting Witness: Ancient Writings on Metal," *Faculty Publications* 5379 (2021): https://scholarsarchive.byu.edu/facpub/5379.

[24] Westbrook and Wells, *Everyday Law in Biblical Israel*, 43; Egyptian written culture around Nephi's time did not require a signature or a witness for sales records to be considered valid. The scribe was

mere existence of a record produced by a known scribe could authenticate a record.[25] An example is a surviving Demotic Egypt divorce certificate from 490 BCE The document states the divorce and ends succinctly: "Scribe. Horuz son of Nes-Hor-pechrat."[26] No seal, signature, or list of witnesses accompany the scribe's name.[27] In these cultures whose literacy rates were a fraction of ours, the concept that a document's validity can *only* be confirmed by witnesses' signatures did not exist.

Egyptian customs are particularly noteworthy in our discussion as archeological evidence suggests that scribes

---

effectively the witness. Indeed, in the seventh century BCE, scribes frequently referred to themselves as "the witness scribe." See John Baines, *Visual and Written Culture in Ancient Egypt* (Oxford: Oxford University Press, 2009), 75–79.

[25] Prior to Nephi's day, though not common, there is recorded use of unsealed records used in court proceedings. Herbert Liebesny, "Evidence in Nuzi Legal Procedure," *Journal of the American Oriental Society* 61, no. 3 (Sept. 1941): 130–42, https://doi.org/10.2307/594500. Contemporary with Nephi many unsealed deposition and settlement records have been identified. For additional discussion, see Shalom E. Holtz, *Neo-Babylonian Court Procedure* (Leiden, The Netherlands: Brill, 2009), chapter 2.

[26] "Papyrus | Museum Number EA10449," The British Museum, accessed February 6, 2023, https://www.britishmuseum.org/collection/object/Y_EA10449; J. E. Curtis and Nigel Tallis, *Forgotten Empire: The World of Ancient Persia* (London: British Museum Press, 2005), 199.

[27] Only a few centuries later some documents do appear to require additional validation. Continuing with For example a certificate of divorce from 283 BCE appears to have the names of four witnesses on the reverse. Nathaniel Reich, "Marriage and Divorce in Ancient Egypt," *The Museum Journal* 15, no. 1 (1924): 54, https://www.penn.museum/sites/journal/1195/.

operated in Israel after Egyptian custom.[28] Nephi also states he was trained in the language of the Egyptians (1 Nephi 1:2). For over a decade scholars have believed Nephi had formal training as a scribe[29] writing in Paleo-Hebrew, Hieratic or Hieratic cursive (Demotic).[30] Texts in the latter style included "contracts, lawsuits and tax receipts."[31] Nephi also demonstrates knowledge of Judean law.[32] Altogether this invites the possibility that he was able to produce legal documents. If 2 Nephi is considered a collection of documents, do those documents

---

[28] Orly Goldwasser, "An Egyptian Scribe from Lachish and the Hieratic Tradition of the Hebrew Kingdoms," *Tel Aviv* volume 18, 2 (1991): 248–53, quoted in John S. Thompson, "Lehi and Egypt," in *Glimpses of Lehi's Jerusalem*, ed. John W. Welch, David Rolph Seely, and Jo Ann H. Seely (Provo, UT: Foundation for Ancient Research and Mormon Studies, 2004), 266.

[29] Noel Reynolds, "Lehi and Nephi as Trained Manassite Scribes," *Interpreter: A Journal of Latter-Day Saint Faith and Scholarship* 50 (2022): 161–215, https://journal.interpreterfoundation.org/lehi-and-nephi-as-trained-manassite-scribes/; Brant Gardner, "Nephi as Scribe," *Mormon Studies Review* 23, no. 1 (Jan. 2011): 45–55, https://doi.org/10.18809/mormstudrevi.23.1.0045.

[30] Neal Rappleye. *Learning Nephi's Language: Creating a Context for 1 Nephi 1:2.* Interpreter: A Journal of Latter-day Saint Faith and Scholarship 16 (2015): 151-159, https://journal.interpreterfoundation.org/learning-nephis-language-creating-a-context-for-1-nephi-12/. Also notice the Caractors document compares favorably with Demotic characters. Ariel L. Crowley, "The Identification of Characters as Egyptian," *Improvement Era* 45, no. 2 (Feb. 1942), 76–80. Cited previously.

[31]Miriam Lichtheim. *Ancient Egyptian Literature: Volume III: The Late Period.* 2nd ed. (Berkeley: University of California Press, 2006): 8, http://www.jstor.org/stable/10.1525/j.ctt1pp5vf.

[32] John Welch, "Narrating Homicide Chiastically," *BYU Studies Quarterly* 59, no. 5 (2020): 151-176, https://scholarsarchive.byu.edu/byusq/vol59/iss5/9.

have significance beyond their religious meaning? For example, Jack Welch demonstrated that 2 Nephi 1-4 assigns lands and designates the future leader of the people.[33] In Nephi's time, the recording is valid because Nephi (likely a scribe) wrote the document.

Neo-Babylonian Depositions

To compare Nephi's writing with contemporary legal documents let us consider various examples. In Neo-Babylonian tradition, documents discovered and used in legal proceedings included certain details. Pertaining to our discussion, official depositions often appear without a seal. Instead, they typically include the speaker's name and a patronym or title. They often include the scribe's name, date and place of composition, and a list persons present who witness hearing the statement. [34] Documents communicating a judge's decision contain seal(s) and those items found in a deposition.[35]

In describing ancient Mesopotamian court proceedings, Shalom Holtz describes four types of recorded depositions: accusatory, testimonial, memoranda, and sworn depositions.[36] There are no identifying markings on court statements to identify them as depositions. This

---

[33] Welch, "Lehi's Last Will and Testament," 61–82.

[34] Holtz, *Neo-Babylonian Court Procedure*, 101.

[35] Ibid., 37.

[36] "Different text-types that record only statements: accusatory depositions, depositions of testimony, memoranda of depositions, depositions under oath. These text-types do not explicitly mention the activities of a court… Although these texts do not describe the entire dispute and decision, many of the statements seem to have been made as part of a larger legal process," see Holtz, *Neo-Babylonian Court Procedure*, 100–116.

contrasts with Old Babylonian times when depositions may begin with the phrase "tablet of confirmation" [37] or "tablet with a sworn statement."[38] Neo-Babylonian depositions begin with "[Personal Name] said thus." Depositions do not describe the entire dispute, nor do they appeal directly to the judge to render a specific decision. They are made before officials or a group of people stating to whom the declarations are made or who was present. Studies suggest that some depositions used in legal cases were made in unofficial settings,[39] court record could also be made outside of official buildings.[40] This may have been out of necessity. It is not likely that all judiciaries had equal access to court rooms (a discussion of judiciaries will follow). Holtz identifies depositions based on their content, inclusion in the legal archive, their references to the case, adjudicating authorities, or audience. Depending on the type of deposition, the scribe may or may not be identified. As their name suggests, only sworn depositions document an oath taken by the speaker. Using Holtz's analysis as a guide, Jacob's, Isaiah's, and Nephi's words in 2 Nephi (2 Nephi 6-10, 12-

---

[37] Martha T. Roth, "Reading Mesopotamian Law Cases PBS 5 100: A Question of Filiation," *Journal of the Economic and Social History of the Orient* 44, no. 3 (2001): 266-267.

[38] Harry Hoffner, "Records of Testimony Given in the Trials of Suspected Thieves and Embezzlers of Royal Property," in *Context of Scripture Vol. III*, ed. William W. Hallo and K. Lawson Younger, Jr. ((Leiden, The Netherlands: Brill, 2003): 57, https://archive.org/details/the-context-of-scripture/page/57/mode/2up.

[39] Holtz, *Neo-Babylonian Court Procedure*, 103

[40] In Assyria "as a consequence of the fact that various administrative officials could act as judges, there was no specific court building." See Karen Radner, "The Reciprocal Relationship Between Judge and Society in the Neo-Assyrian Period," *MAARAV* 12, no. 1-2 (2005): 43.

24, 25-28 respectively) have features that are seen in formal witness depositions.

The lack of surviving First Temple documents makes it difficult to create a detailed taxonomy of writing from that time. Entire genres from that era are likely unknown. It follows that we cannot establish with perfect certainty the precise nature of a text dating from Neo-Babylonian times. However, the characteristics of surviving depositions can support our analysis. Research has shown conclusively that cultures across Mesopotamia, including Israel, significantly influenced neighboring legal systems.[41] In other words, aspects of the legal systems of *surrounding* nations may compare as a surrogate for the legal procedure *within* Judea. The comparison of Nephi's writing with contemporary legal documents is essential. Ancient Near Eastern documents help us detect some legal conventions and language of the period.

Similarities with Neo-Babylonian Depositions

Second Nephi 6 begins with an introduction similar to contemporary witness statements. For example Yale Oriental Series (YOS) 6,131 begins:

> The *mār banî*[42] in whose presence [m]Anim-aḫḫē-uṣur the messenger of the crown prince said thus to [m]Nabû-šarra-uṣur the *ša rēš šarri*[43] administrator of the Eanna:[44]

---

[41] Westbrook and Wells, *Everyday Law in Biblical Israel*, 23-24

[42] Often translated as "citizens" or "freemen"; see Holtz, *Neo-Babylonian Court Procedure*, 54.

[43] High ranking temple administrator.

[44] Holtz, *Neo-Babylonian Court Procedure*, 106.

This is followed by a first-person narration describing three cows being entrusted to another's care. In this excerpt one notes the audience's identification (*mār banî*) and the use of formal titles (messenger of the crown). Holtz notes most depositions did not include a sworn statement or the recording of an oath. Instead of an oath, depositions typically described the *audience* in front of whom the statement was made, as seen in YOS 6,131. The inclusion of the audience is a certifying feature. "A deposition could be taken before a local tribunal... It was recorded under the format: "These are the witnesses before whom ([personal name] stated")."[45] Knowing this convention may increase our understanding of the seemingly trivial words Nephi places in the superscription prior to Jacob's statement. He writes,

> The words of Jacob, the brother of Nephi, which he spoke unto *the people of Nephi* (2 Nephi 6:1).

The mention of the audience (the people of Nephi) may be viewed as the inclusion of witnesses present at Jacob's statement and not merely a historical detail. This tradition was not limited to Babylon. For example, when recording Egyptian "transcripts, the participants and onlookers were put down as witnesses."[46] Biblical superscriptions typically do not mention the audience (a notable rare exception is Deuteronomy 1:1). Therefore, some information in the heading prior to Jacob's words is more

---

[45] Joachim Oelsner, Bruce Wells, and Cornelia Wunsch, "Mesopotamia: Neo-Babylonian Period," in *A History of Ancient Near Eastern Law (2 vols)*, ed. Raymond Westbrook (Boston: Brill, 2003), 922.

[46] Sandra Lippert, "Law Courts," *UCLA Encyclopedia of Egyptology*, 1, no. 1 (Dec. 2012), https://escholarship.org/uc/item/4136j3s7.

characteristic of contemporary legal documents than scriptural text.

Another aspect that makes Jacob's statement more like those found in legal records is the reference to Jacob as the "brother of Nephi." The reference to the speaker's brother has no precedent in biblical superscriptions. Biblical superscriptions typically use a patronym (e.g., The words of Nehemiah the son of Hachaliah; Nehemiah 1:1). Yet, Jacob is not referred to as "son of Lehi"; instead, he is the "brother of Nephi." Such titles *are* found in Neo-Babylonian legal records. For example, in the deposition YOS 7, 10 we read,

> Ḫašdaya, brother of Iddinaya, said thus in the assembly.[47]

Again, we note the inclusion of the audience characteristic of the legal records we have discussed.

Witnesses

Moving past the unique superscription there are other indicators Nephi uses Jacob's words as a deposition. In the following parallelism, it is clear that Nephi views Jacob's words in 2 Nephi 6-10 and Isaiah's words in 2 Nephi 12-24 as witnesses:

> Wherefore, I will send [*Jacob and Isaiah's*] *words* forth unto my children to *prove*…that my words are true…

> Nevertheless, God sendeth *more witnesses*, and he *proveth* all his words. (2 Nephi 11:3)

---

[47] Holtz, *Neo-Babylonian Court Procedure,* 103-104; Shalom E. Holtz, *Neo-Babylonian Trial Records* (Atlanta, GA: Society of Biblical Literature, 2014), 20-23, https://doi.org/10.2307/j.ctt5vjz1s.

This citation presents a parallelism, suggesting that Jacob and Isaiah are both witnesses. Bruce Van Orden writes: "Chapter 11 of 2 Nephi serves to connect the witnesses of Jacob, Nephi, and Isaiah, and it is here that Nephi explicitly applied the law of witnesses."[48] Initial readers of the Book of Mormon noticed Nephi's inclusion of Isaiah to corroborate his own words.[49]

The Law of Witnesses

The law of witnesses as understood by those in the First Temple period and how Latter-day Saints understand it is likely different. A Latter-day Saint may believe the law of witnesses refers to multiple sources establishing spiritual truth. For example, three witnesses testify of the existence of the gold plates from which the Book of Mormon was translated. However, amid a list of civil laws, the law of witnesses appears to be focused on protecting the accused from immediate consequences of violated civil laws. Deuteronomy 17:6 (KJV) states, "At the mouth of two witnesses, or three witnesses, shall he that is worthy of death be put to death; but at the mouth of one witness he shall not be put to death" (also see Deuteronomy 19:15-21). Therefore, this convention (law) was used in judicial settings. Its implementation in the Second Temple period also suggests it was used in judicial settings. The law of witnesses appears modified in Rabbinic literature and

---

[48] Bruce A. Van Orden, "The Law of Witnesses in 2 Nephi," in *Second Nephi, The Doctrinal Structure*, ed. Monte S. Nyman and Charles D. Tate Jr. (Provo, UT: Religious Studies Center, Brigham Young University, 1989), 307–21.

[49] "Nephi...transcribes several chapters from Isaiah by way of corroboration." See John Clark, *Gleanings by the Way* (Philadelphia, PA: W. J. & J. K. Simon, 1842), 279.

Qumran rules but still refers to civil law imposing immediate consequences.[50] Debate exists among non-Latter-day Saint scholars regarding Paul's reference to the law of witnesses in Corinthians. With this background, it is no surprise David Garland argues Paul intends to "take disciplinary action" with "judicial proceeding[s]" upon his return.[51] Although Latter-day Saints may be familiar with the law of witnesses to determine the verity of gospel truths, it appears to be used in legal procedure in Judean culture.

Nephi writes as if justifying his invocation of the law of witnesses. "Behold, my soul delighteth in proving unto my people the truth of the coming of Christ; for, for this end hath the law of Moses been given; and all things which have been given of God from the beginning of the world, unto man, are the typifying of him (2 Nephi 11:4)." By implication, it is perfectly acceptable for Nephi to use or appropriate the legal convention of the law to prove Christ's existence.

Nephi's use of legal convention may be somewhat jarring to modern readers who differentiate between the affairs of church and state. But Nephi reassures the reader. Ultimately because God gave the law of Moses to prove "the truth of the coming of Christ" it follows that Nephi can use civil legal convention for the same purpose. This is especially true as such a separation of civil and moral law imposes one's view "on the text from outside the

---

[50] J. David Woodington, "A Precedented Approach: Paul's Use of the Law of Witnesses in 2 Corinthians 13:1," *Journal of Biblical Literature* 137, no. 4 (2018): 1003–18.

[51] David E. Garland, *The New American Commentary: 2 Corinthians* (Nashville: Broadman & Holman, 1999), 541.

text."[52] Nephi's explanation suggests his society can differentiate between civil and moral law. But there may not be a similar division between the two as we see today. If we accept that Nephi used legal convention to record and document religious matters, he would not be the only one to do so. Nehemiah 10 records several individuals seal a covenant with God. Isaiah 5:3 incorporates a plaintiff statement into his writing, which we will discuss later. Additionally, 4Q365 from the first century BCE demonstrates both biblical text juxtaposed with legal text. Interestingly, "there is no scribal indication [there] is nonbiblical material; the text simply flows out of biblical and into nonbiblical material as if there were no difference between the two."[53]

Comparative Analysis of "Prove" in The Book of Mormon

Nephi states that he delights in proving to his people the truth (2 Nephi 11:4). Ryan Sharp has suggested that because Nephi *also* delights in Isaiah's words, Nephi is using Isaiah's words as a proof.[54] To better understand the Nephite concept of proof, I will turn to comparative analysis. As recorded in Alma 34:6-7 Amulek states Alma, "prove[s]... that the word is in Christ (vs 6)." Amulek is explicit. Alma proved this by "call[ing] upon the words of

---

[52] J. Daniel Hays, "Applying the Old Testament Law Today," *Bibliotheca Sacra* 158, no. 629 (2001): 21-35.

[53] Sidnie White Crawford, *The Text of the Pentateuch: Textual Criticism and the Dead Sea Scrolls* (Berlin: De Gruyter, 2022), 205. Note that on page 8, Crawford refers to this material as "legal." The note was written more recently than the original article.

[54] Ryan Sharp "Except Some Man Should Guide Me: Studying Isaiah with Nephi and Jacob," in *They Shall Grow Together*, 352.

Zenos,... Zenock,... [and] Moses (vs 7)." It appears the cultural understanding of a "proof" in Nephite society refers to the expression of multiple testimonies. This usage is also seen when another prophet named Nephi exposes Seantum as the murderer of a chief judge. Nephi provides a miraculous sign exposing the murderer. However, the sign is not what proved the case. Following a confession, Helaman 9:38 reads that Seantum, "was brought to prove that he himself was the very murderer." The only contribution Seantum made to the case was his testimony. Yet Mormon writes it was *Seantum* who proved the issue. These examples suggest the term "prove" in Nephite society refers to testimony or official statements.

Parallelism and comparative analysis of the term "prove" are some details that show Nephi is using the words of Isaiah and Jacob as witnesses.

Sworn Depositions and Oaths

When depositions were made under oath, surprisingly little notation was used. Typical notation is "they swore," saying: "indeed... (followed by the statement)." At times, the name of a deity was recorded as well. The following is an example from a case regarding a deposit of silver from BM 41663.

> (Lines 9–11) Rīmūt son of Šamaš-lēʾi descendant of Arrabtu swore by Šamaš before the judges and [said] thus:

(Lines 11-12) "I and Ṣillaya are the creditors (with debts) owed by Iddin-[Marduk]. We did not know that silver was depo[sited] with Nabû-šuma-iškun."[55]

I will note that this tablet is sealed with the scribe's seal. This statement depicts two essential aspects of an oath which are a statement of sincerity (authenticating element) and the oath content.[56]

Nephi's rhetoric in 2 Nephi 25:4 and, to a lesser extent 2 Nephi 28:1 have features that are found in contemporary oaths. Blane Conklin writes, "Oaths are generally authenticated either by appealing to a precious entity outside oneself or by calling down a curse." While it is not required to link the oath content and authenticating element an explanation is often expressed with a complementizer.[57] Oath content may contain a protasis (stating the claim) and an apodosis (stating the consequence if the claim is not verified). However, documented oaths rarely include the corresponding apodosis.[58] 2 Nephi 25:4 contains the following:

> *Claim:* I give unto you a prophecy
>
> *Authenticating element* (precious entity): according to the spirit which is in me;

[55] Holtz, *Neo-Babylonian Trial Records*, 138

[56] Blane Conklin, *Oath Formulas in Biblical Hebrew,* (University Park, USA: Penn State University Press, 2011), 5:1–12, https://doi.org/10.5325/j.ctv1bxgzws.5.

[57] Ibid., 46-59

[58] Johannes Hackl, *Der subordinierte Satz in den spätbabylonischen Briefen* (Munster: Ugarit Verlag, 2007), 72-73; See also Bruce Wells, F. Rachel Magdalene and Cornelia Wunsch, "The Assertory Oath in Neo-Babylonian and Persian Administrative Texts," *Revue Internationale des droits de l'Antiquité* 107 (2010): 13-29.

> *Claim restated*: wherefore I shall prophesy according to the plainness which hath been with me from the time that I came out from Jerusalem with my father
>
> *Complementizer*: for behold, my soul delighteth in plainness unto my people, that they may learn.

When an apodosis is elided, the resulting consequence is not entirely clear. For example, despite numerous oaths that swear with the life of a deity, to call a potential curse on the respected third party has not been performed as far as we know.[59] Therefore potential unstated consequences for Nephi may include death (i.e., for being a false prophet) or perhaps an acknowledgment the "spirit" is not "in [him]." These two scenarios are in no way comprehensive. Other consequences might include punishment by the spirit upon which he swore or to provide reparations of that which was lost due to Nephi's testimony. At the very least, it appears Nephi is staking all his credibility on his prophecy.

Nephi's stylized oath also appears functionally equivalent to Judean oaths. A comparable oath is found in 1 Kings 22:14, "Micaiah said, "As the LORD lives, I shall speak whatever the LORD tells me."[60] Nephi makes another oath more typical of the time in 2 Nephi 25:20 but it does not appear to apply to the entire section. He states:

> As the Lord God liveth that brought Israel up out of the land of Egypt, and gave unto Moses power that he

---

[59] Conklin, *Oath Formulas in Biblical Hebrew*, 24

[60] For a discussion and examples of oaths containing only "As the Lord Lives" as an authenticating element please see: Yael Ziegler "'As the Lord Lives and as Your Soul Lives': An Oath of Conscious Deference." *Vetus Testamentum* 58, no. 1 (2008): 117–30, http://www.jstor.org/stable/20504320.

should heal the nations after they had been bitten by the poisonous serpents, if they would cast their eyes unto the serpent which he did raise up before them, and also gave him power that he should smite the rock and the water should come forth; yea, behold I say unto you, that as these things are true, and as the Lord God liveth, there is none other name given under heaven save it be this Jesus Christ, of which I have spoken, whereby man can be saved.

Nephi again attests the oath regarding his prophecy in 2 Nephi 28:1. Nephi writes, "And now, behold, my brethren, I have spoken unto you, according as the Spirit hath constrained me; wherefore, I know that they must surely come to pass." The term "surely" is also consistent with King James wording used to record sworn oaths.[61] Further analysis is complicated as the composition in the original language is not extant.

Neo-Babylonian Legal Procedure and Plaintiff Statements

Aside from those discussed, additional components in 2 Nephi suggest it contains writings informed by legal conventions. These include a plaintiff's statement and the promise of additional proof provided by the plaintiff. Additionally, the inclusion of legal rhetoric mention of sealing the record, and a judgment bar appears to be explicit references to judicial activity.

---

[61] For example, in Isaiah 14:24 we read, "The Lord of hosts hath sworn, saying, "Surely…" Book of Mormon translation tends to follow KJV convention to incorporate "Surely" to indicate an oath. This is demonstrated in 2 Nephi 24:24 and Isaiah 14:24.

Due to the lack of records from Judean and Egyptian legal proceedings of necessity we again must turn to other ancient Near Eastern cultures to understand the conventions that might have held sway in Nephi's time and place.[62] This approach is reasonable, as some conventions were standardized over large regions.[63] After evaluating a series of legal proceedings from multiple cities contemporary to Nephi, Holtz wrote the most common format of plaintiff's statements[64] includes three components. These are:

> A. *Opening* (mention of plaintiff and adjudicating authority)
>
> B. *Quotation of the plaintiff's statement*

---

[62] It is clear that the civilizations in question had significant political influence on each other and the surrounding areas. Hebrew Bible attests to this influence, yet there is not a consensus on the degree of influence biblical law had on Judean state law. See Westbrook and Wells, *Everyday Law in Biblical Israel*, 3.

[63] It appears there was a fair amount of standardization based on consistent practices across multiple regions. For example, plaintiff statements with imperatives were found primarily in decision records when cases originated in higher courts. Whereas records of cases originating in informal settings or in lower courts were less likely to contain a plaintiff statement with an imperative. This tendency was observed in the existing records composed in Babylon, Uruk, Tapsuhu, Sippar, and Bit-sar-Babil dating from approximately 560 BCE to ~550 BCE Another tendency in the imperative is the wording. When the plaintiff appeared with the defendant the imperative was typically, "establish our decision." If the plaintiff appeared alone before the judge the imperative was usually, "Judge my case against [defendants name]." The latter decision records may result in a summons rather than a verdict. Similar notation used across multiple regions suggests a degree of standardization present in Neo-Babylonian times. Holtz, *Neo-Babylonian Court Procedure*, 226

[64] Ibid., 227.

C. *Imperative to authority*

For example, the document YOS 19, 101, written in 545 BCE and discovered in Babylon discusses a decision record from a case that apparently pertains to a misappropriated shipment of dates. This document provides an example of a plaintiff statement. The first lines are translated as follows:[65]

> *Opening:*
>
> (Lines 1–3): ᵐNergal-rēṣūa the slave of ᵐIddin-Marduk said thus to the judges of Nabonidus, king of Babylon.
>
> *Quotation of plaintiff's statement*:
>
> (Lines 3-6) ᵐIddin-Marduk, my master, loaded a shipment of 480 *kur* of dates for transport from the hinterland on the boats belonging to ᵐAmurru-natan, the boatman, son of ᵐAmmaya.
>
> (Line 7) "He had him bear the responsibility for keeping the dates."
>
> (Lines 8-10) "He brought the boats to Babylon and he gave me ᵐIddin-Marduk's message. 480 Gur of dates was written i[n it]."
>
> (Lines 11–12) I took account of the dates, and 47*gur* 1 *pi* were missing.
>
> (Lines 12–14) I raised a claim against ᵐAmurru-natan concerning the missing amount of the dates and . . . thus:
>
> (Lines 14-15) I did not take your dates.
>
> (Line 15) Afterwards, an informer . . .
>
> (Line 16) 4 Gur 1 Pi of dates . . .
>
> (Line 17) and behind my boat . . .
>
> (Line 18) those dates in . . .
>
> (Lines 19–20) We contracted a contract stating thus: ᵐAmurru-natan illegally took 7 *gur* 1 *pi* of dates.

[65] Ibid., 28-29.

(Lines 22–23) After ᵐAmurru-[natan] wrote this contract until today . . .

(Line 24) Now, I have brought him before you.

Imperative to authority:

(Line 25) "Establish our decision!"

The opening statement is demonstrated by mention of the plaintiff and adjudicating authority in lines 1-3. The plaintiff statement is given in lines 3-24. Finally, an imperative to authorities demands a judgment in line 25.

Isaiah uses this format in records that survive in the Bible. For example, in the parable of the vineyard, Isaiah states, "And now, O inhabitants of Jerusalem, and men of Judah, judge, I pray you, betwixt me and my vineyard (KJV Isaiah 5:3)." Additional features of this passage in Isaiah make the allusion to a courtroom explicit.[66] Such explicit allusions to a courtroom suggest plaintiff statements may indicate a degree of specificity. Isaiah summarizes the facts of the case, identifies the adjudicating body, and demands a judgment be made.

One may wonder if Nephi copies Isaiah's pattern here and, therefore, merely happens to copy a plaintiff's statement unknowingly. However, people from various backgrounds used the plaintiff's statement to include slaves.[67] The Bible records cases in Israel that could be held publicly with the citizenry acting as judges.[68] This

---

[66] Shalom E. Holtz, "Praying as a Plaintiff," *Vetus Testamentum* 61, no 2 (Jan. 2011): 258–79, https://doi.org/10.1163/156853311X564796.

[67] See: A Boatman's Fraud HSM 890.4.8 in Holtz, *Neo-Babylonian Trial Records*, 80-82

[68] In Judah, "the king, elders, local assemblies of citizens, state officials and priests could function as judges"; see Wells, *The Law of Testimony*, 19

suggests some aspects of legal proceedings were commonly understood. The same plaintiff statement formula is written near the end of Nephi's record. Nephi states:

> *Opening:*
> I, Nephi, cannot write all the things which were taught among my people; neither am I mighty in writing, like unto speaking; for when a man speaketh by the power of the Holy Ghost the power of the Holy Ghost carrieth it unto the hearts of the children of men... But I, Nephi, have written what I have written... And now, my beloved brethren, and also Jew, and all ye ends of the earth...
>
> *Quotation of plaintiff's statement:*
> [these] are the words of Christ...
>
> *Imperative to authority:*
> And if they are not the words of Christ, judge ye (2 Nephi 33:1-11).

Nephi mentions himself, the audience, and his claim before demanding a decision.[69] This language is consistent with that found in legal records.

An additional characteristic of ancient Mesopotamian court proceedings is the promise of additional proof provided by the plaintiff.[70] This is in sharp contrast to today's convention. In modern times, all evidence must be

---

[69] A point of clarification regarding Nephi's relation to the reader. Nephi addresses the reader with what is termed a "plaintiff statement." In modern times the plaintiff is a person or party wronged by the defendant. Thus, a modern reader might opine Nephi implies the reader has wronged him. However, this is not the convention anciently as state officials often brought suit against the defendant on behalf of the state.

[70] Holtz, *Neo-Babylonian Court Procedure*, 135-165.

presented before a judgement can be made. Holtz notes, "Most of the guarantees for testimony can be shown to be the result of the guarantor's accusations that must be substantiated. In these cases the accusations were made during formal hearings, after which the guarantor assumed responsibility for the testimony" (i.e., by providing another witness).[71] Nephi does this by stating: "Christ will show unto you, with power and great glory, that they are his words, at the last day; and you and I shall stand face to face before his bar; and ye shall know that I have been commanded of him to write these things (2 Nephi 33:11)." Here again Nephi's record is consistent with contemporary legal proceedings.

Nephi is not esoteric. Because Nephi glories in plainness, he may include rhetoric describing his record as a legal document. In the final paragraphs of 2 Nephi he mentions a judgment bar. Nephi's closing verse makes explicit reference to court proceedings. "For what I seal on earth, shall be brought against you at the judgment bar." All twelve mentions of the word "bar" in the Book of Mormon refer to a setting of judgment.

The Reader's Role

The reader's position in this setting is initially ambiguous. Following the implications of this plaintiff's statement, Nephi posits the reader in an adjudicating role. It appears then that the words of Christ themselves are on trial. Nephi writes, "if they are not the words of Christ, judge ye." The reader's role in the proceedings is nuanced.

---

[71] Ibid., 148.

Unlike other prophets in the Book of Mormon, Nephi does not posit God as a judge. When the reader is the defendant, Nephi identifies Christ's words as the judge. Nephi states, "[H]e shall bring forth [H]is words unto them, which words shall judge them at the last day (2 Nephi 25:18)." Restating the point, Nephi writes that the "nations who shall possess [the writings in question] shall be judged of them according to the words which are written (verse 22)." Therefore, in this future courtroom (it appears Nephi is not speaking rhetorically), the reader and the written word assume the roles of both judge and defendant at different times.

While Nephi's allusion to a judgment bar is clear, our relationship with God in the courtroom is more ambiguous. To better comprehend these implications I will discuss ancient judicial structures.

Ancient Near East Judicial Structure

Because of such prevalent legal terms, the context of contemporary legal systems must be considered to interpret Nephi's message.

In Nephi's day, the legal systems of neighboring nations allowed for appeals. Prior to that era, appeals were generally not allowed in Mesopotamia. Leaders had embodied deities and judgments were immutable.[72] To

---

[72] "The judge stands in the place of deity according to the general view prevailing in antiquity. If he fails in the proper discharge of his duties, he lowers the dignity of his office; and the deity, by permitting him to go astray, shows that he no longer desires the judge to speak in his name. Confidence in the probity and ability of the judge is the condition sine qua non of the execution of justice. Defective as this uncompromising attitude toward a judicial error may be from a

appeal a judgement put in question the capability of the leader. Even an attempt to appeal could result in punishment.[73] This was not necessarily impractical, as punishment could be levied for false testimony. However, this stands in stark contrast to procedure in the Neo-Assyrian and Neo-Babylonian kingdoms where, appeal was practiced.[74] The relatively new practice of appeal allowed defendants of the time to criticize lower-court judges. While the king was ultimately responsible for justice, he was less directly involved. This resulted in numerous letters directed to Neo-Assyrian kings complaining of injustice by appointed representatives and subsequent requests for appeal.[75]

---

modern standpoint in not recognising an appeal from a lower to a higher court, the ethical basis is both sound and of a high order. With such a provision… the integrity of the courts was firmly secured for all time." See Morris Jastrow Jr., *Aspects of Religious Belief and Practice in Babylonia and Assyria* (New York: The Knickerbocker Press, 1911), 396.

[73] Ronald A. Veekner, "An Old Babylonian Legal Procedure for Appeal: Evidence from the Ṭuppi Lā Ragāmim," *Hebrew Union College Annual* 45 (1974): 1–15, http://www.jstor.org/stable/23506845.

[74] Karen Radner, "Mesopotamia: Neo-Assyrian Period," in *A History of Ancient Near Eastern Law (2 vols)*, ed. Raymond Westbrook (Boston: Brill, 2003), 887.

[75] "The…way of addressing the ruler is rendered by the Akkadian expression… literally meaning «to present oneself to the king, » i.e., to bring a case to his attention. In messages of this type, supplicants sometimes explicitly ask the king for a judgment (denu epašu) or allude to cases previously decided by the ruler (denuparasu). For all that, it did not mean that the monarch himself pronounced a verdict… the king is never mentioned in [legal proceedings], which is at first sight surprising considering the relatively large number of letters asking for justice….All this seems to show that the Neo-Assyrian kings did not themselves pronounce the verdict in the cases submitted to them, but delegated this task to those whom they deemed competent

Further, appeals were likely needed due to what could be viewed as two legal systems in existence simultaneously. State administrators who were not legal professionals such as treasurers, eunuchs, and cup-bearers could adjudicate cases.[76] In contrast to the modern concept of mediator, these lower judges were state officials. Pierre Villard notes, "There also existed, alongside the notables acting as judges, a specialized judicial administration, directed by two of the highest figures in the state."[77] While this approach involved multiple levels of judges, they all derived their judicial authority from the king and acted as his representatives. Appeals for justice were therefore made by seeking the word of the king.[78] Villard

---

for it. It is therefore understandable why the interventions of the ruler have not left any traces in the judicial documentation, whereas from the point of view of the petitioners, it was indeed the king who had rendered justice to them." Pierre Villard, "Degrees of jurisdiction and the notion of appeal in the Neo-Assyrian period," *Ash-Sharq: Bulletin of the Ancient Near East – Archaeological, Historical and Societal Studies* 6, no. 2 (Nov. 2022): 113–126, https://archaeopresspublishing.com/ojs/index.php/ash-sharq/article/view/1756.

[76] "Other state officials could take on judicial duties but are attested in this role much less frequently than the *sukalla* [vizier] and the *sartennu* [chief judge]. The *masennu* ("treasurer") assumed the role of the judge in a text from Assur (no. 22), and from the fact that he had a court clerk... at his disposal we can infer that also the *rab sa resi* ("chief eunuch") could pass judgment. The *rab saqe* ("chief cupbearer") was supposed to act as judge in the matter of an unsettled debt but somehow failed to do so; according to a memorandum from Nineveh, the king had been approached instead to speak justice." See Radner, "The Reciprocal Relationship," 57.

[77] Villard, "Degrees of jurisdiction," 113–26.

[78] Małgorzata Sandowicz, "Nabonidus and Forty Thieves of Uruk: Criminal Investigation in Neo-Babylonian Eanna." *Iraq* 76 (2014): 245–61, http://www.jstor.org/stable/43307197.

continues, "Neo-Assyrian kings did not themselves pronounce the verdict in the cases submitted to them, but delegated this task to those whom they deemed competent for it... from the point of view of the petitioners, it was indeed the king who had rendered justice to them."[79]

Consistent with the tradition of his day, Nephi does not place God as a Judge. Rather, the *word* of God will judge and Christ will stand by and verify they are his words. In Nephi's judicially inflected writings, when the reader is at the judgement bar of God, the judge naturally should be a representative of God: in this case, the words of Christ. The Hebrew concept of "words" (*dabar*) carries the presumption that words contain their referents' essence or fundamental character. Therefore, the word of the Lord can represent the Lord, just as judges and designated functionaries at the time acted as representatives of the king. Additional meanings of *dabar* include "law" or "reality."[80] The judge could be understood to be God's law or God's reality. Nephi's imperative to the reader is to judge if his words are the words of Christ. It is an imperative to judge if the book of 2 Nephi is God's representative, his law, and his reality. In the process, Nephi explicitly posits the revealed law, expressed in words, as subjugate to God, mirroring the relationship between judicial functionaries and the embodiment of legal authority, the king. While one has the right to appeal

[79] Villard, "Degrees of jurisdiction," 119.
[80] Isaac Rabinowitz, *A Witness Forever: Ancient Israel's Perception of Literature and the Resultant Hebrew Bible* (Bethesda, MD: CDL Press, 1993), 8.

and invoke the word of the King, Nephi assures the reader that his words are God's words.

Differences Between Nephi's Record and Legal Records

It would be irresponsible to omit key differences between Nephi's writings in 2 Nephi and Neo-Babylonian trial records. These include the detail of the writing and the absence of a list of names and seals. These differences do not change the overall interpretation.

First, Nephi appears to be writing a verbatim record whereas extant records appear paraphrastic. Remember that scribes did not act as transcriptionists but played an active role in legal proceedings.[81] For example, the following citation from three witnesses YOS 7,66 reads:

> We were digging below the canal wall, together with ᵐNanaya-iddin son of ᵐInnin-zēra-ibni when we killed 2 ducks, property of the Lady-of-Uruk, from the pen of ᵐNidintu and ᵐGuzānu, sons of ᵐNanaya-iddin, we buried them in mud.

The record continues as a summary:

> The corpses of these 2 birds... were inspected in the assembly... [the assembly judges] decided [the accused]... must pay a 30-fold restitution for the 2 ducks.[82]

In this case, the actual words of the judges are never recorded. The testimonies of *three* defendants are recorded as a *single* statement which is so brief that it may be a

---

[81] Sara J. Milstein, *Making A Case: The Practical Roots of Biblical Law* (Oxford: Oxford University Press, 2021), 35.
[82] Holtz, *Neo-Babylonian Court Procedure*, 49.

summary rather than a verbatim record. Perhaps a contributing factor in Neo-Babylonian record keeping is complications of the medium. The brevity depicted in Neo-Babylonian records is not ubiquitous in the ancient Near East. In the reign of Ramses II a surviving statement from a Theban court appears to include much more detail and may be more likely to be a verbatim recording. Cairo 65739 reads:

> As for myself I am the wife of the district superintendent Simut, and I came to dwell in his house, and I worked in weaving, caring for my clothing. Now in the regnal year 15, in the seventh year of my having entered into the house of the district superintendent Simut, the merchant Raia approached me with the Syrian slave Gemniherimentet, while she was a young girl, and he said to me, "buy this young girl and give to me her price" – so he said to me. And I took the young girl and I gave to him her price. Now look, I am saying the price which I gave for her in the presence of the authorities …[list of items]… And I gave them to the merchant Raia, without there being any property of the citizeness Bakemut among them and he gave to me this little girl and I called her Gemniherimentet by name.[83]

The papyrus goes on to record the judge's response. This case predates the Neo-Babylonian records by several hundred years. I present it as a comparison because existing judicial records from Egypt are rare. Cairo 65739 suggests the records in Egypt were closer to a word-for-word recording. If judicial records were made in Israel, the paucity of extant records suggests they were also

---

[83] Robert Ritner, "A Lawsuit Over a Syrian Slave," in *Context of Scripture Vol. III*, 31-2.

made on a less durable medium (i.e., such as the papyrus observed in Cairo 65739). It is reasonable that less durable material facilitated longer recordings. Therefore while Nephi's lengthy records show differences from some legal records, there appears to be a precedent for more detailed records in legal proceedings.

A second deviation between Nephi's writing and Mesopotamian judicial records is the lack of a list of persons present. In YOS 7,66, the names of the assembled judges are listed following the decision. Likewise in Cairo 65739 the names of six persons present were listed. These persons could attest to the proceedings. Nephi does not list individual hearers of his words. Toward the end of his record he states the words were taught "among [his] people (2 Nephi 33:1)." Additionally, as mentioned, Nephi does state Christ will show unto the reader that they are His words (2 Nephi 33:11). This does have a loose similarity with the legal convention of the time. Those listed at the conclusion of the record can attest to the veracity of the record.

Finally, following the list of names of those present there would often be a seal. Likewise, immediately after mentioning Christ as a witness of the record Nephi states he seals the record. This is a unique feature because books in the Hebrew Bible, as they are presented today, do not contain a seal nor do they mention closing with a seal.[84]

---

[84] A colophon found at the conclusion of a Septuagint Book of Esther serves a comparable function to a seal and could be considered the sole exception. See Sidnie White Crawford, "Where Are All the Colophons? Colophons in the Ancient Near East and in the Dead Sea Scrolls" in *Mighty Baal: Essays in Honor of Mark S. Smith* (Harvard Semitic Studies, Volume: 66, 2020), 101–115.

Yet, in 2 Nephi 33 there is a reference to a seal; however, there is no record of a seal.

Nephi may be referencing the record as inaccessible. *Chatham* in Songs of Solomon 4:12 is understood as locked or inaccessible. Welch writes that Book of Mormon prophets differentiate between 'seal' vs 'seal up.' Nephi's use of the word "seal" likely refers to "physically tying the document shut and affixing a wax or clay seal to the closure." "Seal up," as used in Moroni 10:2 signifies protected or safeguarded.[85]

Many references in the Hebrew Bible to sealed legal documents appear literal (i.e., Jeremiah 32:11-15). The act of using a physical seal in ancient Israel is well-attested. Seals of the time typically had two lines which contained a name and a title or patronym.[86] Legal custom in the surrounding region was to make multiple copies of judicial records. The sealed copy would have the seal(s) of

---

[85] "Jared and Moroni never use the word *seal* (or *sealed*) by itself, while the phrase *seal up* (or *sealed up*) is used eight times (see Ether 3:22, 23, 27, 28; 4:5 [3 times]; and 5:1). By contrast, 2 Nephi 27 uses the word *seal (sealed)* by itself nine times (see verses 7, 8, 10 [3 times], 11, 15, 17, 21), while the expression *seal up (sealed up)* is used only twice (see 2 Nephi 27:8 and 22; in verse 8 its meaning is unclear, but in verse 22 it means "to seal up" in the sense of "to hide up"). The dominance of *seal up* in Ether indicates that "sealing up" something meant something different, especially in the mind of the brother of Jared, from what "sealing" meant for Nephi." Jack Welch, "Doubled, Sealed, Witnessed Documents: From the Ancient World to the Book of Mormon," in *Mormons, Scripture, and the Ancient World*, ed. Davis Bitton (Provo, UT: FARMS, 1998), 428.

[86] Jeffrey Tigay and Alan Millard, "Seals and Seal Impressions," in *The Context of Scripture. Canonical Compositions, Monumental Inscriptions, and Archival Documents from the Biblical World, Vol. 2*, ed. W.W. Hallo and K.L. Younger, Jr. (Leiden, Netherlands: Brill, 2000), 197-204.

the judge(s) present. Copies of the sealed document would include inscriptions of the seal(s).[87] To my knowledge, the manner of sealing contemporary metal records is not described. Metal foundation documents were written without seals and placed within stone boxes underneath or within a building's foundation (footnote 20). Sealed Roman plates have been found.[88]

If Nephi referred to legal convention the seal may have been removed or the seal inscription wasn't included in translation. Regardless, whether Nephi is speaking rhetorically or literally that Nephi mentions sealing the document at the end of the record after naming a witness is certainly reminiscent of the contemporary legal practice we have been discussing. The paucity of books in the Hebrew Bible containing a seal and the simultaneous widespread use of seals in legal records suggest a sealing reference has some degree of specificity for legal texts. In this regard, again Nephi's record is more similar to contemporary legal documents than extant religious writings.

---

[87] Holtz, *Neo-Babylonian Trial Records*, 146.

[88] Two bronze metal plates from the time of Trajan, found in Mainz, Germany… have four holes, two on the corners and two in the middle: "The seal was fashioned in the following manner: A cord made out of bronze wire threads was laced through the middle holes of both plates and the two ends were tied together on the back side of the second plate. Over these knots a film of wax was poured, on which the witnesses impressed their seals. A half cylindrical bronze seal was soldered over the wax for protection." See Welch, "Doubled, Sealed," 403-4

Change of Genre: Revision through Introduction

One may wonder if Jacob and Isaiah intended their text as legal statements. Nephi's explanation of the law of witnesses could be viewed as an apologetic explanation for incorporating them as such. I do not consider their primary intent in this paper.[89] They both may reference legal proceedings. However, it is important to note they would not need to intend their writing as legal statements for Nephi to incorporate them as such.

Sara Milstein documents scribes often revise text through the manner of introduction. Notably, insertions prior to a text can change the genre of the text. Examples of this

---

[89] Jacob, a priest, emphasizes Nephi's role as a king, protector, and the audience's dependence on him for safety (2 Nephi 6:2). He then states his words are "the words which my brother has desired that I should speak unto you (2 Nephi 6:4)." This may be tantamount to declaring himself a messenger of the King. Further, Jacob's audience would have readily recognized the laws among a list of admonitions he cites (2 Nephi 9:30-38). The setting is public, but there is an obvious contrast, for example, with a public case in Alma 10 which involves professional interrogators (vs 31) and the use of public oaths (vs 10). John Thompson interprets Jacob's words as a covenant renewal (the composition includes a preamble and titulary, historical overview and covenant speech proper, stipulations of the covenant or treaty, cursings, and blessings would be seen in a covenant renewal) delivered at a festival celebration. John S. Thompson, "Isaiah 50-51, the Israelite Autumn Festivals, and the Covenant Speech of Jacob in 2 Nephi 6-10." in *Isaiah in the Book of Mormon*, edited by Donald W. Parry and John W. Welch (Provo, UT: Foundation for Ancient Research and Mormon Studies, 1998): 123-150. Similarly, as discussed, Isaiah incorporates explicit legal terminology in the Parable of the Vineyard (Isaiah 5:1-7). He also writes, "Bind up the testimony, seal up the law among my disciples (Isaiah 8:16)." Regardless, Nephi's use of Jacob's words and Isaiah 2-12 does not require they originated as depositions.

include the Community Rule, 1 Chronicles 1-9, the Greek versions of Esther, Deuteronomy 1-3, and Nehemiah 1.[90] If we consider the Judean legal genre (such as Deuteronomy or the Community Rule) legal precepts are prefaced by "general information regarding the covenant."[91] Deuteronomy 5, for example, contains the Ten Commandments. Prior to writing the commandments there is some background framing the setting (vs. 1-5). Considering this genre it appears Nephi intends the book to be three statements (2 Nephi 6-28) prefaced by material introducing the setting (2 Nephi 1-5). I view the three witness statements as the central portion of 2 Nephi.

The Language of Judean Legal Texts and Second Nephi

The general language of extant Judean legal records is also described by Milstein. She offers suggestions of what legal rhetoric may have looked like.[92] Common to many

---

[90]Sara J. Milstein, *Tracking the Master Scribe: Revision Through Introduction in Biblical and Mesopotamian Literature.* (Oxford: Oxford University Press, 2016), 74.

[91] Milstein, *Tracking the Master Scribe*, 65.

[92] Milstein begins by reviewing Old Babylonian scribal school curriculum. She points out that numerous model or practice contracts have been discovered. These were contracts that are copied in order for a scribe to learn a format and appropriate legal phrases. Milstein lists criteria for these practice texts including hurried characters, multiple copies of the document on a single tablet, exaggerated details, increased attention to format and other aspects. She then notes fewer model (practice) court transcripts have been found. This may indicate less scribes practiced the production of court records. Alternatively, there appears to be less focus on standardizing the court records based on a larger amount of intra-record heterogeneity when compared with finished contracts. But as scribes rewrote practice documents some habits developed. Milstein notes legal terms and phrases (more so than

Hebrew legal texts[93] are root variations, colorful features, unusual legal situations, resonance with contracts, emphasis on social roles, repetitive language, and discussion of money or other penalties.

Certainly, in isolation, none of these features can identify a legal text or rhetoric. Scriptural text is filled with such writings. However, because of their prevalence in Judean legal texts, these features likely form a *sine qua non* to identify such a text. If Nephi wrote 2 Nephi with legal proceedings and format in mind, he might have considered using the established legal rhetorical flourishes. These findings are present in 2 Nephi (table 1).

---

formatting) are conserved across practice and official court records in Old Babylon. Some of these patterns are similar to language seen in Old Babylonian pedagogical and court records. This does not indicate that Judean scribes had access to Babylonian records per se but did have access to Babylonian precepts (page 153). Milstein applies the same analysis to Biblical legal records. Many of the laws in Exodus and Deuteronomy are so detailed they appear to be based on cases and pedagogical records. Some laws retain sections of their original cases. For example, Deuteronomy 19:4 is often translated as, "This is the case of…" While aspects of Milstein's work is controversial she successfully shows common traits that appear in these passages. See Sara Milstein, *Making a Case* (Oxford University Press, 2021), 20-158

[93] Specifically Milstein analyzes early sections of the Covenant Code and select laws she terms "Hebrew legal fictions." Ibid., 72.

Feature	Verse
Colorful language	And they shall be visited with thunderings, and lightnings, and earthquakes, and all manner of destructions, for the fire of the anger of the Lord shall be kindled against them, and they shall be as stubble, and the day that cometh shall consume them, saith the Lord of Hosts. 2 Nephi 26:6
Root variations[94]	Lehi counsels his sons to arise from the *dust* (*aphar*) and leave darkness and *obscurity* (*aphel*) (2 Nephi 1:21).[95] Nephi also uses permutations on Joseph's name. Following a prophecy by Joseph we read Laman and Lemuel choose to *increase* (*yasap*) in anger instead (2 Nephi 3-5), resulting in hatred and rejection of the suzerain covenant and freedom.[96]
Unusual legal situations	For the atonement satisfieth the demands of his justice upon all those who have not the law given to them. 2 Nephi 9:26

---

[94] Milstein also noticed extensive wordplay in the HLFs. Some root variations are only observed in the Hebrew case laws suggesting scribes would intentionally seek uncommon words if needed when writing in this genre. Milstein, *Making a Case*, 81.

[95] Jeff Lindsay, ""Arise from the Dust": Insights from Dust-Related Themes in the Book of Mormon (Part 1: Tracks from the Book of Moses)," *Interpreter: A Journal of Mormon Scripture* 22 (2016): 179-232, https://journal.interpreterfoundation.org/arise-from-the-dust-insights-from-dust-related-themes-in-the-book-of-mormon-part-3-dusting-off-a-famous-chiasmus-alma-36/.

[96] Matthew Bowen, "Their Anger Did Increase Against Me": Nephi's Autobiographical Permutation of a Biblical Wordplay on the Name Joseph," *Interpreter: A Journal of Latter-day Saint Faith and Scholarship* 23 (2017): 115-136, https://journal.interpreterfoundation.org/their-anger-did-increase-against-me-nephis-autobiographical-permutation-of-a-biblical-wordplay-on-the-name-joseph/

Resonance with contracts	And they sell themselves for naught; for, for the reward of their pride and their foolishness they shall reap destruction. 2 Nephi 26:10
Emphasis on social roles	They rob the poor because of their fine sanctuaries; they rob the poor because of their fine clothing; and they persecute the meek and the poor in heart, because in their pride they are puffed up. 2 Nephi 28:13
Repetitive language	Wo unto the liar, for he shall be thrust down to hell. Wo unto the murderer who deliberately killeth, for he shall die. Wo unto them who commit whoredoms, for they shall be thrust down to hell. 2 Nephi 9:34-36
Discussion of money or other penalties	For the time speedily cometh that the Lord God shall cause a great division among the people, and the wicked will he destroy; and he will spare his people, yea, even if it so be that he must destroy the wicked by fire. 2 Nephi 30:10

Table 1: Features in Judean legal texts are also seen in 2 Nephi. While many of these features are seen throughout the Book of Mormon, it is essential to demonstrate their presence in 2 Nephi to confirm language consistent with contemporary legal rhetoric.

Legal Reasoning

Shin Hur analyzed legal reasoning in Genesis and Deuteronomy. This is particularly relevant as many place the authorship of much of Deuteronomy in the time of King Josiah (shortly before Nephi leaves Jerusalem).[97] Hur notes cases from that period emphasize conjecture and

---

[97] Shin Wook Hur, *The Rhetoric of the Deuteronomic Code: Its Structures and Devices* (Emory Theses and Dissertations, 2013), 60.

transference (i.e., whether an event happened and with whom lays the fault). Hur based this on the case of Tamar, Achan and Deuteronomy 22:13–21. Less emphasis was placed on qualifying features such as degree of guilt or clarity of the law.[98] This perspective is similar to what we read in Nephi's writings. Nephi is content to cite Isaiah's language, "for shall the work say of him that made it, he made me not (2 Nephi 27:27)?" Nephi also states, "by the law no flesh is justified (2 Nephi 2:5)." To Nephi's audience it appears a person is either 'guilty' or 'not guilty.' Rhetoric of the period depicts cases as 'black' or 'white.' This aspect of early Nephite culture may account for some of the rhetoric a modern reader may find binary.

With that understanding in mind it likely seemed foolish and foreign to Nephi's original audience that the Gentiles of the last days will try to minimize or qualify evil deeds. He states,

> And there shall also be many [in the last days] which shall say … fear God [but] he will justify in committing a little sin; yea, lie a little, take the advantage of one because of his words, dig a pit for thy neighbor; there is no harm in this; and do all these things, for tomorrow we die; and if it so be that we are guilty, God will beat us with a few stripes, and at last we shall be saved in the kingdom of God." (2 Nephi 28:8)

Nephi mentions this to characterize, "false and vain and foolish doctrines" among the Gentiles (2 Nephi 28:9).

---

[98] Ibid., 30-36. Other Judean rhetoric techniques mentioned are also seen in Second Nephi; such as alternating prescription and proscription; "choose eternal life …and [do] not choose eternal death (2 Nephi 2:28-29)."

Presumably, this example resonated with an audience unfamiliar with post-Hellenistic arguments.

Nephi's Conservative and Revisionistic Citations of Isaiah

Nephi's adaptive citations of Isaiah are well described. Scholars note Nephi's writing, "makes additions…omits material in others, transposes, [and] makes grammatical changes."[99] "As might be expected of a truly ancient and authentic record."[100] In contrast, it is not clear that Nephi adapts the text in 2 Nephi 12-24, which appears to be a much more conservative citation. This next section demonstrates Nephi reproduces Isaiah 2-14 using conservative techniques. A possible motive is that Nephi intends Isaiah's words to have formal purpose.

Much of Nephi's Isaiah-centric writing can fairly be described as exegetical.[101] This is not to say that he exceeded his remit as a scribe. Exegetical techniques of the period were accepted and expected as core scribal activities.[102] These included manipulation, harmonization, paraphrasing, allusion, and, in some cases, the addition of new material to expand on existing themes.[103]

---

[99] Sharp, "Except Some Man Should Guide Me," 338.

[100] Ibid.

[101] Grant Hardy, "Prophetic Perspectives and Prerogative: How Lehi and Nephi Applied the Lessons of Lehi's Dream," in *The Things Which My Father Saw: Approaches to Lehi's Dream and Nephi's Vision*, ed. Daniel Belnap, Gaye Strathearn, and Stanley A. Johnson (Salt Lake City: Deseret Book, 2011), 199–213; Hardy, *Understanding the Book of Mormon*, 61-65

[102] Sidnie White Crawford, *Rewriting Scripture in Second Temple Times* (Grand Rapids, MI: William B. Eerdmans Publishing, 2008), 4.

[103] Crawford, *Rewriting Scripture*, 80.

Expansionistic techniques included inflation, glosses of long or complex passages, and synoptic additions.[104] "When Nephi engages with the writings of Isaiah," notes Ryan Sharp, "he is quite comfortable adapting the prophetic record."[105]

To accurately characterize texts from that era, it is helpful to classify them according to scribal intervention. Accordingly, these texts may be categorized broadly as conservative or revisionistic.[106] Such classifications help us more fully appreciate the process by which each text was recorded, and can avoid anachronistic labelling. Of course, not all texts fall neatly into any given category in their long histories. Some manuscripts may come down to us as the result of a mixed treatment.[107] Such a characterization of Nephi's text is especially relevant to our discussion because the accurate rendering of a witness deposition may demand a more conservative approach.

---

[104] Frank Moore Cross, "The History of the Biblical Text in Light of the Discoveries in the Judean Desert" in *Qumran and the History of the Biblical Text*, ed. Frank Moore Cross and Shemaryahu Talmon (Cambridge, MA: Harvard University, 1975), 283. See also Sidnie White Crawford, "Scribal Traditions in the Pentateuchal and the History of the Early Second Temple," in *Congress Volume Helsinki 2010*, edited by Martti Nissinen (Leiden, The Netherlands: Brill, 2012), 148, 167-84.
[105] Sharp, "Except Some Man Should Guide Me," 334.
[106] The latter may also be described as a "free" or "creative" scribal approach. See Sidney White Crawford, "Understanding the Textual History of the Hebrew Bible: A New Proposal," in *The Hebrew Bible in Light of the Dead Sea Scrolls*, edited by N. David et al. (Gottingen: Vandenhoeck & Ruprecht, 2012), 60-69.
[107] Drew Longacre, "A Contextualized Approach to the Hebrew Dead Sea Scrolls Containing Exodus," (PhD thesis, University of Birmingham, 2014).

George Brooke describes five aspects of text written by scribes when performing exegesis (he uses the term "rewritten scriptural text" to define the genre of that time).[108] These include:

1. The source is thoroughly embedded in its rewritten form not as explicit citation but as running text.
2. The dependence of a rewritten scriptural text on its source is also such that the order of the source is followed extensively.
3. The dependence of a rewritten scriptural text on its source is also such that the content of the source is followed relatively closely without very many major insertions or omissions.
4. The original genre or genres stays much the same.
5. The new texts are not composed to replace the authoritative sources which they rework.

Brooke's criteria make clear 2 Nephi 12-24 does not qualify as rewritten while all other citations in 1-2 Nephi are rewritten. Some consider 1 Nephi 20-21 a citation, but that view imposes our modern conventions on the text. Indeed, 1 Nephi 20-21 meets all scholarly criteria for its classification as a *rewritten* scriptural text. Most notably, without a superscription it cannot be considered an explicit citation. This leaves modern scholars at something of a loss as to where Isaiah's words actually start (c.f., Brooke's criterion 1).[109] Additionally, Nephi never states

---

[108] G J. Brooke, "The Rewritten Law, Prophets and Psalms: Issues for Understanding the Text of the Bible," in *The Bible as Book: The Hebrew Bible and the Judaean Desert Discoveries*, ed. E. D. Herbert and Emmanuel Tov (London: British Library, 2002), 32. As summarized by Sidnie White Crawford in *Rewriting Scripture*, 12.

[109] "As Nephi quoted this Servant Song to his brothers, he included several lines of text in the first verse not found in other current versions of the Old Testament. It is not clear whether these additional

that his copy can directly replace Isaiah's words (criterion 5). In contrast, prior to the citation of 2 Nephi 12-24 Nephi suggests his text may replace Isaiah's words (as a copy). He writes, "And now I write some of the words of Isaiah, that whoso of my people shall see these words may lift up their hearts and rejoice for all men. Now these are the words (2 Nephi 11:8)." Another indication that 2 Nephi 12-24 is not an exegetical text is that it is introduced as an explicit citation of Isaiah. "The word that Isaiah, the son of Amoz, saw concerning Judah and Jerusalem (2 Nephi 12:1)." These are two criteria that 2 Nephi 12-24 fails to meet; therefore, only 2 Nephi contains a citation that is not demonstrably exegetical.

---

lines were in the ancient text of Isaiah that Nephi knew, or if these lines are his own commentary." Terry B. Ball, "Isaiah's 'Other' Servant Songs," in *The Gospel of Jesus Christ in the Old Testament* (Provo, UT: Religious Studies Center, Brigham Young University, 2009). See also John A. Tvedtnes, *The Isaiah Variants in the Book of Mormon* (Provo, UT; Foundation for Ancient Research and Mormon Studies, 1981), 73.

Examples of Nephi's Literary Technique

Isaiah 11:4-10	2 Nephi 21:4-10	2 Nephi 30:9-16
but with righteousness shall he judge the poor and reprove with equity for the meek of the earth and he shall smite the earth with the rod of his mouth and with the breath of his lips shall he slay the wicked	but with righteousness shall he judge the poor and reprove with equity for the meek of the earth and he shall smite the earth with the rod of his mouth and with the breath of his lips shall he slay the wicked	**and** with righteousness shall **the Lord God** judge the poor and reprove with equity for the meek of the earth and he shall smite the earth with the rod of his mouth and with the breath of his lips shall he slay the wicked
		for the time speedily cometh that the Lord God shall cause a great division among the people, and the wicked will he destroy; and he will spare his people, yea, even if it so be that he must destroy the wicked by fire.
and righteousness shall be the girdle of his loins and faithfulness the girdle of his reins	and righteousness shall be the girdle of his loins and faithfulness the girdle of his reins	and righteousness shall be the girdle of his loins and faithfulness the girdle of his reins
the wolf also shall dwell with the lamb and the leopard shall lie down with the kid and the calf and the young lion and the fatling together and a little child shall lead them	the wolf also shall dwell with the lamb and the leopard shall lie down with the kid and the calf and the young lion and the fatling together and a little child shall lead them	**and then** shall the wolf dwell with the lamb and the leopard shall lie down with the kid and the calf and the young lion and the falling together and a little child shall lead them
and the cow and the bear shall feed their young ones shall lie down together and the lion shall eat straw like the ox	and the cow and the bear shall feed their young ones shall lie down together and the lion shall eat straw like the ox	and the cow and the bear shall feed their young ones shall lie down together and the lion shall eat straw like the ox
and the sucking child shall play on the hole of the asp and the weaned child shall put his hand on the cockatrice' den	and the sucking child shall play on the hole of the asp and the weaned child shall put his hand on the cockatrice's den	and the sucking child shall play on the hole of the asp and the weaned child shall put his hand on the cockatrice's den
they shall not hurt nor destroy in all my holy mountain for the earth shall be full of the knowledge of the Lord as the waters cover the sea	they shall not hurt nor destroy in all my holy mountain for the earth shall be full of the knowledge of the Lord as the waters cover the sea	they shall not hurt nor destroy in all my holy mountain for the earth shall be full of the knowledge of the Lord as the waters cover the sea
and in that day there shall be a root of Jesse which shall stand for an ensign of the people to it shall the Gentiles seek and his rest shall be glorious	and in that day there shall be a root of Jesse which shall stand for an ensign of the people to it shall the Gentiles seek and his rest shall be glorious	**wherefore, the things of all nations shall be made known; yea, all things shall be made known unto the children of men**

Table 2: Selected Examples of Nephi's Citation of Isaiah. From Royal Skousen, *The History of the Text of the Book of Mormon* Part 5 The King James Quotations in the Book of Mormon. Provo, UT: Foundation for Ancient Research and Mormon Studies, 2019 and *The Book of Mormon: the Earliest Text.* These excerpts appear to demonstrate Nephi's use of conservative and revisionistic scribal techniques.

To get a sense of the fidelity with which Nephi treats 2 Nephi 12-24, we can compare it to a corresponding section in 2 Nephi 30. Fortunately, we have a section of Isaiah that Nephi cites twice (table 2). While acknowledging the limits of textual criticism across translated texts, if we assume the English translation has *any* degree of correlation with the base text, then it does appear that these two passages appeared differently as Nephi wrote them. However, because analysis of Dead Sea Scrolls shows early written texts existed in multiple parallel versions,[110] it is possible Nephi has multiple versions of Isaiah on the brass plates.

However, based on the conventions of the time, I would expect Nephi to change Isaiah's words in 2 Nephi 30. Surrounding 2 Nephi 30 there is evidence of inner scriptural exegesis which meets all five criteria identified by Brooke mentioned above.[111] Whatever Nephi's motivations behind the difference between 2 Nephi 21:4-

---

[110] Emmanuel Tov, *Textual Criticism of the Hebrew Bible: Revised and Expanded Fourth Edition* (Minneapolis: Fortress Press, 2022), 15.

[111] Using the above criteria, first, 2 Nephi 30:9-16 is embedded without defining where Isaiah's words start or stop. Second, much of the order of 2 Nephi 30:9-16 follows that of Isaiah 11. Third, there are no major insertions. Fourth, the subject matter of Isaiah 11 and 2 Nephi 30 are similar. Finally, there is no suggestion that 2 Nephi 30 replaces Isaiah's words.

10 and 2 Nephi 30:9-16 (table 2), only the latter text is firmly exegetical.

Let us consider Nephi's situation. Nephi values Isaiah's words, but his children do not understand Isaiah (2 Nephi 25:1-3). Nephi seeks to preserve Isaiah's words for his people (2 Nephi 11:8). An easy way to resolve this dilemma would be to modify Isaiah's words. Nephi has the tools to do this, but Nephi appears not to do so in 2 Nephi 12-24. The data in table 2 suggest that Nephi needed *both* to comment on this text *and* change a few words. Instead of placing comments in 2 Nephi 21, which would risk compromising the record, Nephi re-writes these verses in a later section. This suggests Nephi will not allow even minor changes to the record in 2 Nephi 12-24. Such fidelity, we would expect with a document with a formal extrinsic purpose,[112] such as a certified copy or a verbatim deposition. Considering the textual freedom enjoyed by scribes in Nephi's day, it seems clear that they copied text verbatim as a deliberate choice.

---

[112] Supporting the notion 2 Nephi has a more formal purpose is the introduction of words attributed to others as well. We discussed 2 Nephi 6:1 states, "The words of Jacob, the brother of Nephi." This verse serves no important narrative purpose: we have already read about Jacob in 1 Nephi 18, 2 Nephi 2 and 5. The reader knows Jacob is Nephi's brother. While we can never be sure of Nephi's reason for reintroducing Jacob, his choice connotes a level of formality not previously apparent in his writings. Nephi did not introduce his father's visions or blessings with such formality. This sudden formality is unusual for someone modern readers have described as a guide. Joseph Spencer, *1st Nephi: A Brief Theological Introduction* (Provo, UT: The Neal A Maxwell Institute for Religious Scholarship, 2020), 119. Another example of such formality is 2 Nephi 12:1 and 23:1.

Distribution of Variants

Certainly, textual analysis is best performed in a text's original language.[113] As Nephi's original writings are not available presently, we are left to compare KJV Isaiah with *The Book of Mormon: The Earliest Text*.[114] This is not an entirely expedient choice: scholars have found evidence to suggest that the language of the King James Bible is the language or base text of the Book of Mormon.[115] While a full discussion of this relationship is beyond the scope of this paper, it is clear that the King James Version is our closest available analog to Nephi's English text. Given the amount of Isaiah's writings in Nephi's text—more than 400 verses—these two works lend themselves to quantitative comparison. Drawing on three sources, I will compare 2 Nephi 12-24 to other sections of Isaiah found in Nephi's writing.

Royal Skousen has dutifully reconstructed the earliest text of the Book of Mormon from all known sources. Using this text, he identified the closest edition of the King James Version used as a base text. Skousen defined a

---

[113] Arie van der Kooij, "Review: Eugene Ulrich and Peter W. Flint, Qumran Cave 1.II: The Isaiah Scrolls: Part 1: Plates and Transcriptions; Part 2: Introduction, Commentary and Textual Variants. DJD 32.," *Dead Sea Discoveries* 22 (2015): 116–17.

[114] Royal Skousen, ed., *The Book of Mormon: The Earliest Text*, 2nd ed (New Haven: Yale University Press, 2022).

[115] "The base text for the Isaiah quotations in the Book of Mormon is indeed the King James Version of the Bible." Royal Skousen, "Textual Variants in the Isaiah Quotations in the Book of Mormon," in *Isaiah in the Book of Mormon*, 369–90. For more discussion, please see 32:00–38:00 of "History of the Text of the Book of Mormon - Royal Skousen - Volume 3 Parts 5 and 6 - 1/15/20," Scripture Central, March 5, 2020, video, 1:33:19, https://www.youtube.com/watch?v=4jlPgeX0U3Y.

citation when sixteen identical words appear consecutively in both texts.[116] Skousen then identified all textual variations within those citations.[117] He published this data. All words not occurring in the analogous text were printed in bold font. For example, the four words "O house of Israel" in 2 Nephi 7:2 are in bold font because this phrase is not found in Isaiah 50:2. Similarly, minor variants are also bolded. For example, "water" is considered different from the plural "waters."[118] I tabulated all the words Skousen identified in each section. 4.1% of the words in 2 Nephi 12-24 were bold. In other sections of the Book of Mormon 12.0% or 14.7% of the words are bold (figure 1). It is clear 2 Nephi 12-24 has only a third the rate of bold text (corresponding with variants) compared to other KJV citations in the Book of Mormon. While there are many possible causes for the discrepancy in these proportions, a possible contributing cause is changing between conservative or revisionistic scribal techniques. Many of the KJV citations in the Book of Mormon are exegetical (revisionistic) as they meet Brooke's criteria and are not meant to replace their corresponding texts. These generally exegetical texts have bolded words 14.7% of the time in Skousen's findings. The exegetical text by Nephi has a similar proportion (12%). However, 2 Nephi 12-24 contains text that is seemingly closer to its KJV analogue.

---

[116] Royal Skousen, "The History of the Book of Mormon Text: Parts 5 and 6 of Volume 3 of the Critical Text," *BYU Studies Quarterly* 59, no.1 (2020): 19.

[117] Ibid., 289-431.

[118] Ibid., 304.

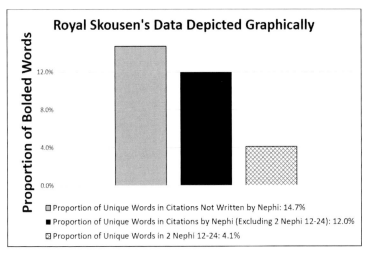

Figure 1. The Proportion of Unique Words in *The Book of Mormon: The Earliest Text* Compared with Analogous Text from the Closest *King James Bible* Base Text. Data compiled from pages 289-431 of Royal Skousen *The History of the Text of the Book of Mormon Part 5: King James Quotations.* Total word count and bolded words (representing a change in the Book of Mormon text) were tabulated. This method does not account for omissions, only material unique to the Book of Mormon within that section. 911 of 6,196 (14.7%) total words were bolded in Jacob to Moroni. 462 of 3,858 (12.0%) total words were bolded in Nephi's record excluding 2 Nephi 12-24. 310 of 7,537 (4.1%) total words were bolded in 2 Nephi 12-24. The proportion of changes in Nephi's citations (excluding 2 Nephi 12-24) is similar to other sections of the Book of Mormon which are typically exegetical.

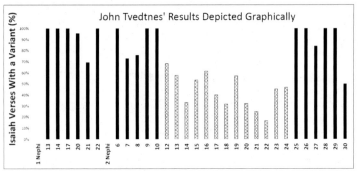

Figure 2. Percentage of Isaiah Verses Containing a Variant in Nephi's Writing. Data was compiled from pages 6-24 of John Tvedtnes *The Isaiah Variants in the Book of Mormon*. Results are displayed by chapter. Hatched marks indicate Nephi's conservative citation of Isaiah. Within 2 Nephi 12-24, 126 of 275 (46%) verses demonstrated a variant. This is compared to all other Isaiah citations in Nephi's writing (solid) that showed 116 of 141 (79%) verses had a variant.

John Tvedtnes' work offers a second approach to the same comparison.[119] After a manual comparison by two reviewers,[120] Tvedtnes documented all variations between multiple versions of the Isaiah and Nephi texts. He found 416 verses "cited" in the first and second books of Nephi. The criteria for citation was reviewer consensus. Figure 2 shows the incidence of variants by chapter. In 2 Nephi 12-24 he found that 46% of verses contained minor variants. In all other Isaiah citations 79% demonstrate a variant.

---

[119] John A. Tvedtnes, "Isaiah Variants in the Book of Mormon," in *Isaiah and the Prophets: Inspired Voices from the Old Testament*, ed. Monte S. Nyman and Charles D. Tate Jr. (Provo, UT: Religious Studies Center, Brigham Young University, 1984), 165–78.

[120] These reviewers looked at Hebrew Masoretic text, the Hebrew scrolls found at Qumran (notably 1QIsa, which contains all sixty-six chapters), the Aramaic Targumim, the Peshitta, the Septuagint or Greek translation, the Old Latin and Vulgate, and the Isaiah passages quoted in the New Testament. Ibid.

More recently Ann Madsen published a comparison of Isaiah variants found in Nephi's writings.[121] Her methods varied from Tvedtnes as she was able to incorporate much of Skousen's critical text findings.[122] Her results were nearly identical to those of Tvedtnes. She found variants in 50% (137/275) of 2 Nephi 12-24 verses. Outside those chapters she reports 86% (96/111) of verses had variants (Tvedtnes found 46% and 79%, respectively). For readability, her publication does not include some verses where Isaiah is cited on multiple occasions partially accounting for the minor difference in total verse count.[123]

Thus, *all three studies*—Skousen's word-by-word comparison, Tvedtnes', and Madsen's manual evaluations of variants at verse level demonstrate that 2 Nephi 12-24 is closer to the corresponding Isaiah KJV text than other Isaiah citations. While this data may appear convincing, these data are significantly limited in that they do not attempt to measure causality. For that, we must rely on context. The differing rates of variants may suggest that one or more sections en bloc were systematically treated

---

[121] Ann N. Madsen and Shon D. Hopkin, *Opening Isaiah: A Harmony* (Provo, UT: Religious Studies Center, Brigham Young University, 2018).

[122] Royal Skousen, *Analysis of Textual Variants of the Book of Mormon* (Provo, UT: Foundation for Ancient Research, 2006).

[123] On the surface, there may appear to be a disagreement in these results. Skousen's data showed a 3-fold difference in variation between the sections in question. Madsen's and Tvedtnes' findings result in less than a 2:1 difference in the variant incidence. However, the latter works are based on the number of verses with a variant. Skousen's data allowed for a more granular analysis. The ratio difference suggests that areas with higher variation by verse also have more variants within each verse.

differently (intentionally or otherwise) than its corresponding analog.

Context surrounding high-variation areas corresponds with exegetical writings, and context surrounding low-variation areas suggests a more conservative scribal approach. Thus, Nephi's conscious decision to leave aside exegetical techniques and cite Isaiah verbatim may have contributed to the discrepancy in variant rates.[124] An attempt to classify Nephi's writings on the same terms as other contemporary literature further supports the view that 2 Nephi 12-24 is a conservative citation.

I propose that Nephi places Isaiah's words as a witness. Other Isaiah "citations" found in Nephi's writings qualify as re-written or revisionistic, a known practice in Nephi's time; this is one possible explanation for the unequal distribution of variants noted above.

To understand 2 Nephi the question is not limited to the existence of a *lengthy* Isaiah citation, or to an en bloc decrease in *rate of variants*. We must also ask why a *firmly non-exegetical*, and therefore conservative, text is found in 2 Nephi.

---

[124] This analysis also suggests that we should be hesitant to regard as citation every verse in the Book of Mormon with an analog in the KJV. This represents something of a novel view: some long passages that are nearly universally considered as "citations"—such as 1 Nephi 20-21—have as much as three times more unique content than that found in other Isaiah-bloc analogs which are equally referred to as "citations."

Second Nephi 4-5: Reactions to the Covenant Renewal

If one views the initial chapters of 2 Nephi as part of a covenant or covenant renewal, it follows the participant's reaction should be recorded. The events following covenant renewals are often recorded. For example, following the Mosaic covenant, the elders of the people saw God and ate (Exodus 24:11). After a covenant renewal performed by Jehoiada, the people "slew Mattan the priest of Baal (2 Kings 11:17-18)." Similarly, after the Lehitic covenant is presented, Nephi details his own commitment as well as Laman and Lemuel's rejection of the covenant. All parties had grievances and had anger with each other at one point. In 2 Nephi 5 the anger of Laman and Lemuel will eventually lead to hatred and a breach of the covenant.

Martin reminds us the term "curse" is covenantal language and signifies Laman and Lemuel made and broke a covenant (a curse can only apply if the covenant is made and breached).[125] Nephi writes, "Because of their cursing which was upon them they did become an idle people, full of mischief and subtlety (2 Nephi 5:24)." In future chapters Nephi will expound on this and state the Lamanites will eventually be subjugated by the Gentiles (2 Nephi 26:15). Much of 2 Nephi depicts the motives and results of not keeping the covenant. The Lamanites will see violence, great bloodsheds, hatred, and become loathsome and captive to the devil. Ultimately it seems Nephi is aware "anger would determine their eternal

---

[125] Martin, "The Prophet Nephi," 117

destiny."[126] Following the covenant renewal in the first chapters of 2 Nephi one expects to read whether the covenant was accepted or not. Instead of unity a schism took place.

The psalm of Nephi is in this section of the text and serves as an attestation of Nephi's commitment following the covenant renewal. An *inclusio* demarcates the text and emphasizes his point. Immediately preceding Nephi's psalm Nephi introduces the topic of anger. He states, "Not many days after [Lehi's] death, Laman and Lemuel and the sons of Ishmael were *angry* with me because of the admonitions of the Lord (2 Nephi 4:13)." Nephi was also *angry*. He asks, "Why am I *angry* because of mine enemy (vs. 27)?" Nephi suggests anger is the "enemy of [his] soul (vs. 28)" and resolves to "*not anger again* (vs. 29)." Nephi chooses God and will prosper in his endeavors. "My God will give me, if I ask not amiss (2 Nephi 4:35)." In attestation Nephi writes, "My voice shall forever ascend up unto thee, my rock and mine everlasting God (vs. 35)." In marked contrast the end of the *inclusio* reads, "But behold, [Laman and Lemuel's] *anger did increase* (2 Nephi 5:2)." Alternatively, Laman and Lemuel will be "cut off from the presence of the Lord (2 Nephi 5:20)." Thus Nephi juxtaposes two parties that experience anger but have two different outcomes. This contrast also brings to mind the two choices Nephi had

---

[126] Matthew Bowen, "Their Anger Did Increase Against Me": Nephi's Autobiographical Permutation of a Biblical Wordplay on the Name Joseph," *Interpreter: A Journal of Latter-day Saint Faith and Scholarship* 23 (2017): https://journal.interpreterfoundation.org/their-anger-did-increase-against-me-nephis-autobiographical-permutation-of-a-biblical-wordplay-on-the-name-joseph/

mentioned previously: liberty or captivity (2 Nephi 2:27). To choose anger results in captivity.

In response to the Lamanite's rejection of the covenant (and resulting subjugate state) God will again reach out offering liberty. Nephi uses permutations of 'Joseph' (*yosip* and *yasap*) in these sections to link the prophecy of Joseph, anger and the eventual restoration of Israel. Nephi resolves to "anger *no more* (*yosip*), Laman and Lemuel choose to *increase* (*yasap*) in anger. This led to hatred, severance from God and subjugation. Because of the Lamanite's eventual state the Lord will need to set himself *again* (*yosip*) (2 Nephi 6:14) to redeem his people. This is the fulfillment of *Joseph*'s prophecy in 2 Nephi 3.

Yet, in no way does Nephi over-emphasize Joseph's role in the covenant (2 Nephi 25:21). With permutations of Judah's name Nephi intertwines the role of the children of Joseph and Judah in eventually keeping the covenant. Nephi writes the Jews bring salvation, yet the Gentiles do not "remember the travails, and the labors, and the pains of the Jews" in bringing forth the Bible and salvation. Nephi writes, "What thank they (*yodu*) the Jews (*et-hayyehudim*)?" playing on both the meaning and phonemes of the terms. Additional meaning can be seen in the combined use of travails and salvation as these suggest Jewish history embodies the Suffering Servant (2 Nephi 29:4).[127]

---

[127] Matthew L. Bowen, "What Thank They the Jews"? (2 Nephi 29:4): A Note on the Name "Judah" and Antisemitism," *Interpreter: A Journal of Latter-day Saint Faith and Scholarship* 12 (2014): 111-125.
https://journal.interpreterfoundation.org/what-thank-they-the-jews-2-nephi-294-a-note-on-the-name-judah-and-antisemitism/.

Considering the first chapters of 2 Nephi as a covenant renewal suggests Nephi's psalm is a response and is therefore not spontaneous.[128] It is an intricately devised record referencing his and other parties' reactions to the covenant. Later, we will discuss 2 Nephi may be part of a sealed document. If that is the case, it is likely a summary of a more extensive document which would further suggest the record is not spontaneous.

Nephi's psalm also stays within the scope of a legal genre. A characteristic of Mesopotamian legal narratives is to incorporating multiple viewpoints.[129] The psalm of Nephi subtly depicts Nephi's feelings. As a component of the covenant, consider Lehi designates Nephi as a leader (2 Nephi 1:28). It is around this time that Lehi also dies. Nicholas Frederick notes a phrase in Nephi's psalm, "Oh wretched man that I am" (2 Nephi 4:17) is identical to Paul's statement in Romans 7:24 (KJV).[130] Frederick suggests this is a "carefully integrated phrase"[131] and that we can profitably compare the two stories. These citations occur when both individuals are at a crossroads. Paul is losing the Mosaic law as a guide and now must rely on

---

[128] Some have suggested Nephi's Psalm is spontaneous. Based on the *inclusio* on each side of Nephi's Psalm it can be viewed as addition. Gardner suggests it is spontaneous; see Gardner, "Labor Diligently to Write," 161.

[129] Cornelia Wunsch, "Legal Narrative in Neo-Babylonian Trial Documents. Text reconstruction, Interpretation and Assyriological method," in *Law and Narrative in the Bible and in Neighboring Ancient Cultures*, eds. K.-P. Adam, F. Avemarie, N. Wazana and D. Felsch (Tubingen: Mohr Siebeck, 2012), 7.

[130] Nicholas Frederick, "The Language of Paul in the Book of Mormon," in *They Shall Grow Together,* 207.

[131] Frederick, "The Language of Paul," 206.

combating sin in a different way (without clear black and white rules). Similarly, Nephi is facing the loss of Lehi his father and long-term guide. The prospects of leading a divided and murderous people are on his mind. Nephi and Paul appear to feel the weight of relying on the spirit's guidance more than ever.

Altogether 2 Nephi 4-5 documents people's response to the covenant. It contains an *inclusio* highlighting the role of anger in rejecting the covenant. It sets up wordplay to connect how the Lord will again set his hand to rescue the people despite this rejection. Nephi moves forward with trepidation and humility. Nephi's psalm also appropriately contains Nephi's feelings, attestation, and reasoning for following the Lord.

The Purpose of Nephi's Second Book

Up to now, I have argued Nephi's second book is a legal document. In modern times connotation may cause us to view legal records as burdensome documents resulting in obligations and penalties. Far from a bureaucratic device depicting contractual terms, Nephi appears motivated to use Isaiah's words in gathering Israel. Following the citation of Isaiah, Nephi employs nearly an entire chapter to the coming forth of a book that will be influential in restoring Israel (2 Nephi 27).

To understand how this book will restore Lehi's posterity to its gathered state, we must first consider one of the Lord's strategies. Nephi states that the children of Israel "swear by the name of the Lord, and make mention of the God of Israel, yet they swear not in truth nor in righteousness (1 Nephi 20:1)." It seems that the Lord has a problem. Israel's children continually state that they will obey his word, but do not follow through on their pledge. They "do not stay themselves upon the God of Israel (1 Nephi 20:2)." God mentions at least two strategies here.

First, He will predict events: He declares things and then shows their completion. God inspires prophecies and demonstrates their fulfillment. The Lord does this because He knows that Israel is "obstinate" and may claim idols brought the acts about (1 Nephi 20:4-5). While Isaiah gives and records many signs (e.g., Isaiah 8) many of Isaiah's words can be interpreted as references to a "local (though still international) series of events."[132] Nephi expands upon this prophecy depicting it "as a series of global events of universal import"[133] that will eventually culminate in Israel's gathering. The importance of a verifiable record cannot be understated. The words of a book play a key role in the Lehitic Covenant.[134] The importance Nephi places on this book is reminiscent of Lehi's words; As Lehi was dying (2 Nephi 3:25) he said to one of his sons, "Wherefore, because of this covenant thou art blessed; for [thy children] shall hearken unto the words of the book. (vs. 23)" These are far from the only references to a pivotal book.

---

[132] Joseph M. Spencer and Jenny Webb, *Reading Nephi Reading Isaiah: 2 Nephi 26-27* (Provo, UT: Maxwell Institute Publications 2016), 64.
[133] Ibid.
[134] The Lehitic covenant consists of four basic elements: 1. A promised land is given to the children of Lehi (2 Nephi 1:5). 2. Prosperity in the land is predicated on obedience to the commandments (Jarom 1:9). 3. Lehi's seed will never perish (2 Nephi 25:21). 4. A record will bring Lehi's seed to a knowledge of their covenant (Enos 1:13, 16; Ether 4:17). Ibid.

Second, aside from prophecies and fulfillment, the Lord declares new things that were hidden and unknown (1 Nephi 20:6). Thus, both fulfilled prophecy and new information are aspects of God's attempts to reconcile Israel with their word and oaths. We can perhaps understand Nephi's purpose from Mormon's perspective. He values 1-2 Nephi and writes these words are pleasing because he, "know[s] that as many things as have been prophesied concerning us down to this day have been fulfilled, and as many as go beyond this day must surely come to pass (Words of Mormon 1:4)." Jacob describes his record in a similar manner. His words speak "concerning things which are, and which are to come (2 Nephi 6:4)."

Nephi states he writes so the reader may *rejoice* (2 Nephi 11:8), *be persuaded* to believe in God (1 Nephi 6:4), and *know God's intent* is to make the reader, "mighty even unto the power of deliverance (1 Nephi 1:20)." Presumably these are the purposes of Nephi's books and the use of legal conventions in 2 Nephi. Nephi writes in the best way he knows how to help the reader affirm the prophecies are true.

Nephi includes Isaiah's prophecies that Assyria will destroy Northern Israel (Samaria). He also includes a prophecy that Assyria will not destroy Jerusalem. Assyria shall, "remain at Nob that day (2 Nephi 20:32)." Continuing in 2 Nephi 20, we find a prophecy of the destruction of Assyria. From Nephi's perspective, these things have come to pass.

Nephi appears to follow the example of Isaiah. He continues with his "own prophecy" (2 Nephi 25:7) and includes new information and predictions. His prophecy includes the destruction of Babylon; some Jews will be carried to Babylon, and then the Jews will return to Jerusalem (vs.10-11). Nephi prophesies of Christ's crucifixion and resurrection and that Jerusalem will be destroyed again (vs. 14). He also predicts the timing of Christ's first coming (vs.19). Hauntingly, Nephi also predicts the destruction of his own people (2 Nephi 26:7).

Many nations rise and fall. Predicting details beforehand is remarkable but perhaps not as impressive as aiding and helping such nations. Nephi shows that woven throughout Isaiah's prophecies are recurrent references to a remnant. Israel is different than other nations because after Israel falls it not only has a viable remnant but upon the restoration of that remnant salvation will be brought to gentiles.[135] Ultimately Nephi viewed the purpose of his record as contributing to the preservation and gathering of Israel (the children of Joseph at the very least). Nephi writes, "wherefore, for this cause hath the Lord God promised unto me that ... which I write shall be kept and preserved, and handed down ... that [Joseph's] seed should never perish (2 Nephi 25:21)."

Overall, as a legal record, 2 Nephi keeps with God's strategies to reclaim Israel by *predicting* events and then *showing* their completion (1 Nephi 20:3). This view stresses the important role prophecy and information will play in the gathering of Israel. To be convincing crucially, Isaiah and Nephi's words *predate* their predictions. It follows that Nephi intends to make a verifiable record using legal conventions.

---

[135] Joseph M. Spencer, *The Vision of All*, 219.

Deutero-Isaiah

With the above in mind we can now understand the significance of finding Deutero-Isaiah in the Book of Mormon. Deutero-Isaiah is a literary construct based on diligent literary analysis; since the 18th century, scholars have hypothesized that Isaiah chapters 40-55 form a distinct entity written more than a hundred years after the life of Isaiah.[136] Because some consider Deutero-Isaiah to have been written after many of the events it prophecies, passages ascribed to that entity have been described as a "retroactive legitimation of the prophetic message."[137] Such an interpretation would appear to compromise the Lord's strategy. A full discussion of Deutero-Isaiah lies outside the scope of this paper. However, several factors relevant to the discussion of Deutero-Isaiah also affect our understanding of 2 Nephi.

Deutero-Isaiah is generally dated after 550 BCE primarily because it refers to the Persian king Cyrus (590-529 BCE) anonymously and by name.[138] Other considerations suggesting this view consider that much of Deutero-Isaiah is written from the perspective of Babylon's destruction and the emphases on rebuilding Jerusalem. Its themes also differ from the rest of Isaiah. Isaiah 1-39 warns Israel of its imminent danger and prophesies of its destruction. In comparison, Deutero-Isaiah contains "nothing but prophecy of salvation."[139] It also seems to cite material

---

[136] Rainer Albertz, *Israel in Exile: The History and Literature of the Sixth Century B.C.E.* (Atlanta: Society of Biblical Literature, 2003), 378.
[137] Ibid., 387.
[138] Ibid., 379.
[139] Ibid., 380.

that may have been written in response to the Babylonian exile.[140] Other themes (such as the "servant of the Lord") and vocabulary (such as "redeemer") are unique within the book to Deutero-Isaiah as well.[141] Deutero-Isaiah has a shift in narrative voice. Finally, its syntax and grammar are consistent with Late Biblical Hebrew, not the Classical Biblical Hebrew in which the rest of Isaiah is written.[142]

Regarding authorship, it has been proposed that a prophet or circle of disciples dedicated themselves to building upon Isaiah's original writings.[143] Because the language found in Isaiah 40-55 is not Priestly or Deuteronomistic,[144] and because it features substantial incorporation of Psalms, it has been proposed that Deutero-Isaiah was composed by temple singers.[145] The prominence of Zionistic themes points to the possibility temple personnel were authors of Deutero-Isaiah.[146]

The notion of textual adaptation may run counter to our modern preconceptions of the way a sacred text should be

---

[140] Ibid., 368.

[141] Joshua Sears, "Deutero-Isaiah in the Book of Mormon: Latter-day Saint Approaches," in *They Shall Grow Together*, 368.

[142] Ibid., 368.

[143] D. Michel, "Deuterojesaja," in *Theologische Realenzyklopädie* (Berlin: Walter de Gruyter, 1981), 521.

[144] Albertz, *Israel in Exile*, 379.

[145] Claus Westermann, *Isaiah 40-66: A Commentary (The Old Testament Library)* (Louisville, KY: Westminster John Knox Press, 1969), 8.

[146] Albertz, *Israel in Exile*, 381; Many theories suggest there was a core that underwent multiple expansions. Naturally there is disagreement in which verses belong to which sections. For example, some posit the initial verses in Isaiah 49 were part of a later addition. Albertz writes, "we must … insist that at the least the Servant Song in 49:1-6 was an indispensable part of the very first edition of the book of Deutero-Isaiah." See Albertz, *Israel in Exile*, 394.

transmitted. But as we have discussed throughout this paper, adaptation of the source text was a common and *expected* scribal activity. "No one form of the biblical text could be said to be preferred before the late first/second century CE."[147] This includes texts produced in religious centers. "The creative/revisionist scribal approach was just as welcome in the Jerusalem temple as the exact scribal approach," argues Crawford.[148] In this light, the idea that temple psalmists may have added a verse here or there should not trouble modern readers. Such modifications presumably made the text more meaningful to the author, orator, and audience. Notwithstanding those advantages, a potential problem arises when texts claim to contain predictions and prophecy. Clearly, when a text is continuously updated it is difficult to determine *what* was predicted and *when*.

Nephi's Record as a Witness for Isaiah's Writings

Setting aside how Nephi viewed his record we need to discuss what the text means to us today. Ultimately, because he left Jerusalem around 600 BCE, Nephi's writings support a pre-exilic date of composition for the portions attributable to Deutero-Isaiah.

It is reasonable to conclude changes were made to Isaiah's text during the post-exilic period, and these could certainly support the dating of Deutero-Isaiah to a later period. It is another thing altogether, however, to suggest that Deutero-Isaiah did not exist in *any* form prior to the Babylonian destruction. Crawford contends in a discussion of biblical texts generally:

---

[147] Crawford, *The Text of the Pentateuch*, 112, 136.
[148] Ibid., 145

Each biblical book reached a recognizable shape at the end of its redactional process, and that shape governed the activity of the scribes who transmitted it going forward... For example, the shape of Exodus began with the Israelites in Egypt...the text within that shape was not fixed, but the shape itself was stable... Thus, even though Exodus exists in two literary traditions (proto-rabbinic and pre-Samaritan) it is recognizably Exodus in both editions.[149]

Because biblical books tend to retain their shape, the existence of Deutero-Isaiah in 2 Nephi suggests Nephi had access to an early version (shape) of the text.[150] The exact phrases and terms will vary based on scribal tradition and translator constraints.

Second Nephi as a Modern Harmonized Text

As we have discussed, the KJV is the base text of the Book of Mormon. The translator of the Book of Mormon incorporated citations from the New Testament. It is, therefore, difficult to imagine reluctance in drawing on sections of KJV Isaiah for Nephi's writings. Like New Testament passages, the wording of these translations may appear anachronistic. Under a "creative and cultural" translation model,[151] a translator may have had

---

[149] Ibid., 115

[150] It is important to note Nephi's writings omit sections of Deutero-Isaiah that represent its most demonstrable anachronisms. For example, Cyrus is not mentioned by name and the culmination of text written from the perspective of Babylon's destruction (Isaiah 47) is not cited.

[151] Many aspects of *The Book of Mormon* suggest it was translated using a "cultural and creative translation model," suggesting that the translator was aware of the reception of the text and modified the text accordingly. See Daniel C. Peterson and Royal Skousen, "A Critical

good reason to produce a text familiar to its intended audience rather than a strictly literal translation. Royal Skousen writes:

> All of this quoting from the King James Bible is problematic, but only if we assume that the Book of Mormon translation literally represents what was on the plates. Yet the evidence…argues that the Book of Mormon translation is tied to Early Modern English, and that even the themes of the Book of Mormon are connected to the Protestant Reformation, dating from the same time period. What this means is that the Book of Mormon is a creative and cultural translation of what was on the plates, not a literal one. Based on the linguistic evidence, the translation must have involved serious intervention from the English-language translator, who was not Joseph Smith. Nonetheless, the text was revealed to Joseph Smith by means of his translation instrument, and he read it off word for word to his scribe. To our modern-day, skeptical minds, this is indeed "a marvelous work and a wonder." [152]

I find the evidence of a creative and cultural translation compelling. Skousen's model of the translation process may be controversial, but it is akin to the process of harmonization performed by ancient Judean scribes. Harmonization is the integration of multiple textual traditions.

One of dozens of examples suggesting the Book of Mormon is not a literal translation is found in 3 Nephi 12:15. The KJV is quoted as, "Do men light a *candle*?" A

Text," The Interpreter Foundation, last modified January 11, 2020, https://interpreterfoundation.org/a-critical-text/; Skousen, "The History of the Text of the Book of Mormon," 212.

[152] Skousen, "The History of the Text of the Book of Mormon," 6.

literal translation should read, "Do men light a *lamp*?"[153] Such a translation can make the text more relatable to its readers. *Yet*, portions of the 1829 English translation of Nephi's writings represent variants *absent* from the KJV and *are* found in the Septuagint,[154] or only in the Great Isaiah Scroll.[155] This suggests the translator by no means disregarded Nephi's record completely. Rather, the translator went between the texts and incorporated the parallel records into a single text.

Regardless of *why* the translator used the KJV and Nephi's record, the practice is reminiscent of Judean scribal behavior we have been discussing. As far as we can tell scribes did not favor one text over another when citing or harmonizing texts.[156] Scribes would cite multiple sources even within the same document. As an example, in the production of 4Q175 a scribe incorporated both proto-Masoretic and pre-Samaritan textual traditions. Such harmonized scriptures were "considered valid scripture

---

[153] Ibid.

[154] Alma Allred, "*The Bible and The Book of Mormon*," FAIR, accessed August 31, 2023, https://www.fairlatterdaysaints.org/archive/publications/the-bible-and-the-book-of-mormon.

[155] Donald W. Perry and Stephen David Ricks, "Worthy of Another Look: The Great Isaiah Scroll and the Book of Mormon," *Journal of Book of Mormon Studies* 20/2 (2011): Article 7. For additional discussion on nine such examples: 2 Nephi 8:5, 8:11, 24:32; Mosiah 15:29, 3 Nephi 20:32; Skousen, *Analysis of Textual Variants*; 594, 597, 760, 803. 1 Nephi 20:11 and 2 Nephi 7:2 13:9, 19:9, 24:32; Donald W. Perry and Stephen David Ricks, *The Dead Sea Scrolls: Questions and Responses for Latter-Day Saints* (Provo, UT: Foundation for Ancient Research and Mormon Studies at Brigham Young University, 2000), 44–46.

[156] Of note excerpted texts "were never recopied." See Crawford, *The Text of the Pentateuch*, 269.

passages since they were used in phylacteries."[157] Similarly, incorporating the KJV in Nephi's translation allows *horizontal* interaction between the textual traditions.

Because the KJV is based on the Masoretic textual tradition ultimately our translation of the Book of Mormon incorporates Judean (e.g., Deutero-Isaiah) textual traditions. Further, because of the integration of early Protestant language and themes[158] that textual tradition is also incorporated. Finally, given multiple Pauline phrases -we have only discussed one- early Christian texts are incorporated as well. The translation of 2 Nephi we have access to can be read as a harmonized text incorporating Nephite, Judean (Masoretic), early Protestant and early Christian textual traditions. There is consensus among scholars that quoting a source indicates authoritative or scriptural status.[159] Therefore those who view the Book of Mormon as sacred may consider the translator's methods a tribute to the validity of the various traditions. Certainly, human errors or omissions occur in all records, but by no means is the effort of hundreds of anonymous scribes and transmitters set aside. Rather, it is incorporated.

I have attempted to demonstrate Nephi's intentions while *writing* 2 Nephi. I propose he intended it to read as a legal document. However, another thing altogether is the

---

[157] Crawford, *Rewriting Scripture in Second Temple Times*, 34-36.
[158] Royal Skousen, "Tyndale Versus More in the Book of Mormon," *Interpreter: A Journal of Mormon Scripture* 13 (2015): 1-8, https://journal.interpreterfoundation.org/tyndale-versus-more-in-the-book-of-mormon/.
[159] Crawford, *Rewriting Scripture in Second Temple Times*, 8.

analysis of the *translation* we have. I agree with Skousen's view of the translation process but it complicates the thesis of this paper. I suggested the minimal variants in 2 Nephi 12-24 compared with other portions of Nephi is due to *Nephi's* desire to produce a verbatim record and to limit his adaptation of the text. Instead, we must consider Nephi's words, the effects of Judean scribes, and the effects of the translator(s) of Nephi's writings. Numerous causes could affect the distribution of variants (e.g., perhaps the translator(s) relied more heavily on the KJV for a particular section or, as we discussed, exegetical changes by any party).

Harmonization and translation process aside, because the general content of a text typically remains intact, inclusion in Nephi's writings suggest he had access to an early version of what we call Deutero-Isaiah. Changes in terminology and grammar are *expected scribal activity* as well as other previously mentioned exegetical techniques. Later "leaving … archaisms in spelling and grammar... became the fashion in Greece and Rome."[160] As Israel returned from Babylon with new Hebrew dialects they likely read and sang the celebratory half of Isaiah much more than the first section that prophesied destruction. Considering the people's history and well-described practices involved in textual transmission we reasonably *expect* anachronistic findings and expansions in pre-exilic texts. The content of Nephi's translation suggests material and themes found in Deutero-Isaiah existed prior to the

---

[160] Paul Wegner, *A Student's Guide to Textual Criticism of the Bible: Its History, Methods and Results* (Westmont, IL: IVP Academic, 2005), 52, 64.

Babylonian exile.[161] Our current translation appears to harmonize Nephite and post-exilic Judean records.

Sealed Records

If Nephi did intend 2 Nephi as a legally permissible record containing Isaiah's words to validate his own writing, it is ironic the text we have today is harmonized (though that doesn't necessarily delegitimize it) and witnesses to Isaiah's words. However, we have not fully considered the cultural practices associated with legal documents. Legal documents of that day were written at least twice. One copy was for public view and another for safe keeping to be opened in need of court proceedings.

In his paper *Doubled, Sealed, Witnessed Documents: From the Ancient World to the Book of Mormon,* Jack Welch notes the word *sepher* (often translated as 'book') even in the singular can refer to both sealed and unsealed copies of the same document. He writes, "Nephi could sometimes speak of that doubled book as a single document."[162] I do not mean Nephi refers to a sealed analog of 2 Nephi in 2 Nephi 27. Rather, Nephi clearly understands a sealed document to be a document with two parts. This applies to our discussion since the final verse of 2 Nephi references "seal[ing]" the record. This may signify its legal authority and place 2 Nephi in a genre of doubled-books. In other words 2 Nephi may point to a second (sealed) copy that includes more content.[163]

---

[161] Joseph M. Spencer, *The Vision of All*, 292-4.

[162] Welch, "Doubled, Sealed," 421.

[163] Welch also differentiates between Book of Mormon terminology for "sealed" vs. "seal up." The latter is more commonly used by the later prophets in the Book of Mormon and means hidden and under the

"The second part of many double documents was not [always] a verbatim repetition of the first part."[164] Unsealed portions contain as little as a quarter of the sealed copy's text. Before Hellenistic influence in Judah the primary or "controlling document" was the sealed portion.[165] Regardless of Nephi's meaning, our lack of access to Nephi's entire body of work, and perhaps even to a literal translation of his writings, is analogous to long-standing limitations on access to full, sealed records.

Similar scenarios appear to be common to all gospel ages. The Israelites did not have access to the tablets containing the Ten Commandments, as they were sealed in the Ark of the Covenant.[166] Rather, they were only able to directly view copies that were man-made and likely less visually impressive.[167] Welch mentions long-held tradition that

---

protection of God. Alternatively, the term *seal* by itself is more commonly used by Nephi and may refer to a double document. Ibid., 426-430

[164] Ibid., 400 . Welch also states, "some of the double documents have a "greatly abridged [*stark verkümmerter*] scriptum interior" from Elisabeth Koffmahn, *Die Doppelurkunden aus der Wüste* Juda ((Leiden, The Netherlands: Brill, 1968), 13.

[165] Ibid.

[166] Further designating their authoritative status, [the tablets] were effectively sealed in the Ark of the Covenant. Official records were generally sealed by the scribe and a second unsealed version was made available for viewing. There was a "'double-document' convention in ancient Near Eastern scribal practice, where an official version remains sealed (or otherwise inaccessible) while a public copy could be consulted, examined, and studied." Mark Leuchter, "Sacred Space and Communal Legitimacy in Exile: The Contribution of Seraiah's Colophon (Jer 51: 59–64a)," in *The Prophets Speak on Forced Migration*, ed. Mark J. Boda et al. (Atlanta: SBL Press, 2015), 94.

[167] The tablets in the Ark do "not come out … again. From now on, the words inscribed in the tablets of stone are hidden words"; see G. J.

even King David had not read the sealed book of the law (thus implying that he was missing aspects of the law). Sealed documents, including much of what Moses wrote, were never distributed.[168] Similarly, the Nephites maintained records whose distribution was forbidden (Alma 45:9). The Jaredites had information that was not distributed (Ether 3:21). As discussed above, Nephi also differentiates between "words which are not sealed" and "things which are sealed (2 Nephi 27:8,15)." Nephi does promise that we will get access at the appropriate time: "And the day cometh that the words of the book which were sealed shall be read upon the house tops (2 Nephi 27:11)." Nephi wrote, "wherefore, the things of all nations shall be made known; yea, all things shall be made known unto the children of men (2 Nephi 30:16)."

If this is the case our copy of 2 Nephi was never intended (by Nephi) to be the controlling or primary document. Rather, it points to a sealed document. This tradition continues in our time, and it is entirely appropriate, for now, that we do not have access to Nephi's sealed

Venema, *Reading Scripture in the Old Testament: Deuteronomy 9-10; 31 - 2 Kings 22-23 - Jeremiah 36 - Nehemiah 8* (Leiden, The Netherlands: Brill, 2004), 36.

[168] "In Jubilees 1:5–29, Moses was given two stone tablets and was shown a vision of "what was in the beginning and what will occur in the future (compare Moses 1)." He was instructed to write a book containing everything the Lord would tell him on the mountain so that it might serve as a testimony in the future against the people. While the Testament of Moses and the book of Jubilees do not say that this eschatological and prophetic book of Moses would be sealed, the authors of those works presume that those writings of Moses would be preserved until the final day of judgment." See Welch, "Doubled, Sealed," 420.

record.[169] Returning to our original thesis, if we consider 2 Nephi as a legal text, it also follows that a second copy - likely lengthier - exists.[170]

Second Nephi Summary/Conclusion

The Book of Mormon was translated without punctuation or extensive formatting. This lack of formal features can sometimes make it difficult to know *what* we are reading. Second Nephi contains an agreement (2 Nephi 1-4) followed by a record of the participant's reactions (2 Nephi 4-5) followed by three witness statements (2 Nephi 6-10, 12-24, 25-28) followed by a plaintiff statement (2 Nephi 33).

Nephi's allusions to sealing the record and to a bar of judgement, his discussion of the law of witnesses, his reference to Isaiah and Jacob as witnesses, formatting and verbiage consistent with Neo-Babylonian depositions and

---

[169] The Lord appears to state additional writings of Nephi exist. He refers to 1 and 2 Nephi as the, "first part of the engravings of Nephi (D&C 10:45)." Decades after his estrangement from the church, David Whitmer—who saw the golden plates from which the Book of Mormon was translated in the presence of an angel and multiple witnesses—commented on the sealed portion, emphasizing that there remained sealed records "of Nephi" that will come "when the time comes." That certainly may refer to other sealed records of Nephi (i.e., not a sealed version of 2 Nephi). As quoted in Lyndon W. Cook, *David Whitmer Interviews: A Restoration Witness* (Orem, UT: Grandin Book Company, 1991), 20–1.

[170] Discussing other sealed and doubled documents Welch writes, "the abridged text served as a working summary or general identification of the main contents of the transaction, so the shortened text would only prevent falsification of the main document in a limited number of cases. In any event, "both texts are always formatted in the same way and written in the same hand." Welch, "Doubled, Sealed," 400.

plaintiff statements, practices used in Neo-Babylonian legal procedures such as requesting an initial judgment be made in the absence of but with the assurance of additional future evidence, vocabulary, paronomasia, reasoning, and finally the inclusion of lengthy non-exegetical text together are idiosyncrasies of 2 Nephi. A possible explanation is that Nephi is using legal convention.

While all the records on metal plates were likely construed in the aggregate as a witness by the Nephites, the unique formatting of 2 Nephi argues strongly that it should be viewed as a witness on its own merits based on legal convention.

Nephi's Optimism

Nephi closes his record with a prayer that many of us, if not all, may be saved in the kingdom of God on the great and last day. This strikes me as interesting because Nephi has seen the wickedness and destruction of Jerusalem, the crucifixion of Christ, and the destruction of his people. At the time of his writing, he is warring with the people now called Lamanites. And yet he prays and genuinely believes that most of us, perhaps all of us, will be saved. Nephi appears to believe that until the last day there is no chasm too deep, nor any desert too remote to disallow a return to full fellowship with God. Indeed, that is one theme found in each section of the triad of witnesses. Nephi proves to us and all readers that we are not cast off forever. God intends to save all people both Israelites and Gentiles.

Nephi tells us that he wrote these words so his people could rejoice. The Nephite populace who experienced the unnerving loss of civilization upon leaving Jerusalem and whose typical daily worries included existential threats could put their minds at rest and know with surety that God lives, loves them, and has a plan.

The Rebuilding and Restoration of Jerusalem

Continuing along the theme of redemption, Nephi consistently returns to one enormously important topic. Forty years after leaving Jerusalem and Nephi seems to think of little but rebuilding the city, which stands as a restoration of his collective children to the knowledge of God. Though Nephi left Jerusalem in body, it seems his heart remained there.

From thousands of miles away, one might think that Jerusalem would have faded into distant memory; a mass grave of people, unfortunately, lost forever. But far from forgetting Jerusalem, Nephi makes it the focus of the witnesses from Jacob and Isaiah. Aside from that, in the narrative portions of Nephi's writings, he manages to somehow make almost every story about gathering Israel.

When Nephi describes the death of his father Lehi, he includes Lehi's dying words to his son Joseph about…the gathering of Israel.

The few extra chapters at the end of 1 Nephi are about…the gathering of Israel.

In the first chapters of 1 Nephi, Nephi recounts his vision of the tree of life. That vision dovetails into…the details and mechanisms behind the gathering of Israel. Are we sensing what is important to Nephi?

Though Nephi talks about the restoration of Israel, he states that he is actually talking about the Messiah. So **for**

Nephi, it seems it is the New Jerusalem that vindicates the Savior, that both identifies the Messiah and defines our role with him. The redemption of Jerusalem is so essential to Nephi that he states if the Lord had not been merciful to him and show him "those who are at Jerusalem," he would have "perished also." It seems that Nephi is so distraught over the cities and nations he has seen destroyed that only a vision of gathered Zion can reassure him.

This echoes Ezekiel. "Ye shall see their way and their doings: and ye shall be comforted concerning the evil that I have brought upon Jerusalem, even concerning all that I have brought upon it. And they shall comfort you when ye see their ways and their doings: and ye shall know that I have not done without cause all that I have done in it, saith the Lord God."

Nephi could not be comforted until he saw the New Jerusalem. This was similar to Jacob's declaration, "for because of faith and…great anxiety, it truly had been made manifest unto us concerning our people, what things should happen unto them…wherefore, we knew of Christ and his kingdom, which should come." For Nephi and Jacob, Christ and the restored Jerusalem are inextricably connected. One cannot exist without the other.

To drive this point home, I have created a list of terms associated with the gathering of Israel. Almost every related term I looked at is used more frequently by Nephi than by other authors of the Book of Mormon.

For example, Nephi writes about 20% of the Book of Mormon but is responsible for 64% of the times Israel is mentioned. He is responsible for 60% of all uses of the term Gentile. He mentions Zion roughly four times more frequently than other prophets as well. If there is one thing Nephi cares about, it is the rebuilding of Jerusalem. Words that are almost exclusive to Nephi's writing include isle, island, Ephraim, Messiah, Judah, and Jew. Of the 45 times Zion is mentioned in the Book of Mormon, Nephi is responsible for 35.

Terms Associated with the Gathering of Israel

Isle:	12 mentions (100%)
Island:	3 mentions (100%)
Ephraim:	11 mentions (92%)
Messiah:	29 mentions (90%)
Judah:	19 mentions (86%)
Zion:	35 mentions (78%)
Jew:	72 mentions (78%)
Manasseh:	2 mentions (66%)
Israel:	138 mentions (64%)
Gentile:	87 mentions (60%)
"That day":	43 mentions (50%)
Jerusalem:	77 mentions (47%)
Joseph:	22 mentions (46%)
Inheritance:	23 mentions (39%)
Remnant:	22 mentions (34%)

Terms Used More Frequently by Nephi Than Other Book of Mormon Prophets (% of total mentions). Nephi wrote about 22% of the Book of Mormon.

So, what does this Zion look like to Nephi? For that answer I need to discuss some literary features first.

Despite writing in Egyptian, Nephi appears to use Hebrew patterns of grammar, including many types of parallelism.

Selected types of Parallelism:

(from "Preserved in Translation" by Donald Parry, 2020)

* Synonymous
* Antithetical
* Coordinating
* Extended
* Number

(Parry, 2020)

For instance, antithetical parallelism places opposing ideas back-to-back to create a strong, meaningful contrast. A straightforward example is found in 2 Nephi 9:39, which reads:

> Remember, to be **carnally minded is death**, and to be **spiritually minded is life** eternal.

In that phrase "carnally minded" corresponds with its opposite "spiritually minded." Likewise "death" stands in sharp contrast to "life eternal."

Remember, to be *c*carnally-minded is *d*death,

opposites

and to be *e*spiritually- minded is*f*life *g*eternal.

Antithetical Parallelism

Antithetical parallelism is a very basic but effective tool. It drives home its central point and makes ideas more memorable. Awareness of this pattern can change our interpretations of some statements. Take the following:

> In as much as ye shall **keep my commandments ye shall prosper in the land**; and in as much as ye will **not keep my commandments ye shall be cut off from my presence.**

2 Nephi 4

4 For the Lord God hath said that:
> *a*Inasmuch as ye shall keep my commandments
> ye shall prosper in the land;
> and
> inasmuch as ye will not keep my commandments
> ye shall be cut off from my presence.

"Prosper" and "Cut Off from God's Presence" are Opposite Concepts

These lines appear to present opposing concepts. Just as the opposite of keeping the commandments is failing to keep them, to prosper is to be in the Lord's presence. By implication, one cannot be in the Lord's presence and fail to prosper. I'm afraid that I misunderstood this verse for years. On a cursory read, it seems to imply that the righteous will become wealthy. Indeed, many Christians to this day associate wealth and righteousness, partly because of their interpretation of verses like this. Such readings may amount to putting the cart before the horse: later on, Mormon states that the just Nephites become rich because of their "steadiness," (Alma 1:29) not the other way around.

Digging a bit deeper, the word "prosper" didn't mean to become rich in the 1830s. The 1828 Webster's Dictionary reports, "to favor; to render successful; to be successful; to succeed." Webster gives an example. "All things concur to prosper our design." So, "to prosper" means much, much more than simply accumulating riches. To prosper is to be successful in whatever endeavor one undertakes. It is not until more recently that the word takes on a pointedly economic meaning, as in "especially to achieve economic success."

When we read Nephi with parallelism in mind, we see that he likely means that to be in the Lord's presence is, among other things, to be successful at our chosen endeavors.

Is this principle shown in the narrative? Yes, it is. Eventually, Laman and Lemuel failed to heed the word of God and do the things they needed to earn the right to independent divine revelation, and so Nephi became a principal source of teaching for them. Finally, after continuing to ignore the Lord, they were cut off from his presence.

But what about Nephi's people? They were in Nephi's presence. What happened to them?

Nephi taught. He taught his people about woodworking and processing iron, copper, brass, steel, gold, silver, and precious ores. Those elements and alloys are mentioned in 2 Nephi 5:15. The point is Nephi *taught*. Among other things, he taught the intricacies of woodworking and metal production.

Aside from that, **Nephi built.** He built a temple, for starters, that allowed the people to have direct access to the Lord. Thereby, Nephi continued Moses' work toward making an entire nation of priests and priestesses. As Lehi had done, Nephi gave some initial instructions to his children. But then Nephi takes extra steps to make sure his people are directly and independently connected with their Heavenly Father. To drive this point home in 2 Nephi 33, Nephi explicitly tells his people to receive revelation for themselves.

Above all, Nephi teaches and empowers. That is the very definition of good. For Nephi, absolute truths govern our lives, though they may be hard to find. His definition of "good" rests on determining the laws of the reality around oneself in order to become capable and prosperous in any way one intends. Nephi knows there is no space in which there is no kingdom, and there is no kingdom in which there are no physical laws. Nephi makes it his business to know and teach all manner of spiritual and physical laws or interactions. This includes everything needed to empower mankind. Laws of language, history, hunting, agriculture, building, spiritual well-being, meditation, mechanical engineering, chemistry, and navigation are good and essential according to Nephi. I believe that Nephi would probably say the same thing Joseph Smith wrote. "The glory of God is intelligence."

In fact, you can't read the first page of Nephi without picking up on the central importance of teaching in his life. 1 Nephi 1:1 states, "I Nephi having been born of goodly parents. **Therefore I was taught…"** Little wonder that Nephi wanted to "preserve the language of his fathers." As we mentioned earlier, there is knowledge in words.

Up to now, I have tried to extrapolate Nephi's definition of "good" from what I make of his writings. I believe that Nephi would say God is good because he empowers others. God gives knowledge and helps others succeed. To be in his presence is to enjoy those blessings. This does not take away from the love one would also feel in God's presence. Nephi writes that to feel the love and support of God is most desirable above all things and the most joyous to the soul.

What is Nephi's Philosophy? What is Good? What is Bad?

Let's build on our initial observations to get a more detailed sense of Nephi's ethics. Second Nephi 2 gives us a look into his conception of good and evil.

In this world, according to Nephi, God develops our agency. This is what Nephi calls the "way." We must choose the way to liberty and freedom and persist in that freedom.

According to Nephi, there are two basic types of things in this universe: things to act and things to be acted upon.

God is intent on making us capable adults able to act within a galaxy infinitely full of various forces.

To develop our agency—or the ability to act for ourselves—we must have:

- choices or alternatives
- delayed natural consequences which follow comprehensible laws
- enticement by opposing forces

The consequences of our actions must be delayed somewhat. If all actions have instantaneous results, we risk developing a sort of Pavlovian conditioning that causes us to react predictably and unthinkingly to various forces. Instead, we need to learn to define problems, consider multiple solutions, weigh the pros and cons of each, make a choice, and persevere until we achieve the outcome we desire. Delayed consequences, even those that are only partially responsive to our decisions, allow this to happen. This is what Nephi calls the law affixed that answers the "ends of the atonement."

Nephi also writes, "Wherefore, man could not act for himself save it should be that he was enticed by the one or the other." After all, we need to uphold our own will under every circumstance. In an environment with infinite influences, our goals will face distraction, boredom, fatigue, bribery, despair, anger, poverty, setbacks, saboteurs, peer pressure, and other influences. If we cannot overcome these distractions, our desires will be overwhelmed by prevailing forces or petty whims.

If it were not for these sorts of weighty choices, we would have no chance to grow. Nephi writes "all things must needs be a compound in one; wherefore...they must needs remain as dead." Nephi is comparing a state of permanent naivety and ineptitude to a sort of death! In other words, remaining ignorant is a fate equivalent to death.

According to Nephi, that is the world we live in. We are all constantly becoming experts in all aspects of agency. In the broad view, this process answers the ends of the atonement. Nephi's philosophy states that developing agency isn't part of the plan, it **is** the plan. **The whole point of everything, including the fall.**

This may be a lot to take in. To look at it from another angle, one Nephite said of the fall, "and now... our first parents were cut off both temporally and spiritually from the presence of the Lord; and thus we see they became subjects to follow after their own will."

To put it yet another way, how many kids would steal a cookie from the kitchen while their parents were staring right at them? There's simply no point: the punishment would be immediate and inevitable. Children who do the right thing in that situation aren't making ethical decisions—they're not using their agency. Similarly, the fall is essential for men and women to have and develop agency.

Because this feels uncomfortable to most people, Nephi assures us that all things were "done in the wisdom of him who knoweth all things." I would like to point out that these concepts are presented as a matter of fact, not as a sort of groundbreaking revelation. Whenever a prophet in the Book of Mormon adds something to doctrine, it seems they write something like, "I have prayed much to know...." Or "this was made known to me by the angel..."

But 2 Nephi 2 is written as if the author is just summarizing and rehashing established truths.

Recall that Nephi states the book of Moses is on the brass plates. It seems likely the following content was present on his copy of the book of Moses. Moses records the Lord describing the people destroyed by the flood. The Lord said, "Behold these thy brethren; they are the workmanship of mine own hands, and I gave unto them their knowledge in the day I created them; and in the Garden of Eden, gave I unto man his agency; and unto thy brethren have I said and…given commandment that they should love one another…but behold they are without affection and they hate their own blood." The Lord goes on to speak about how these will be redeemed.

As far as I know, only Latter-day Saints believe that mortals are essentially embryonic gods developing agency. When God said in Genesis, "Man is become as one of us to know good and evil." Latter-Day Saints do not perceive him as mocking Adam or speaking ironically. I am not sure why, but the destiny of becoming a god is a bold concept to some people, even an unpopular one. I consider this the exact concept that Abinadi was killed for asserting in Mosiah 7:27. This is what was meant when he said that "Christ…should take upon him the image of man" **and** that "man was created after the image of God."

It is this view that encourages Latter-day Saints to esteem Eve so highly. It was Eve's vision to accept a path to agency. And it was her brave soul that took the first steps toward fulfilling God's plan. It is no wonder that Eve is recognized as "glorious" in canonical Latter-day Saint texts.

Nephi goes on to say that "because we are redeemed from the fall we have become free forever knowing good from evil; to act for ourselves and not to be acted upon."

Recall that God values his children extraordinarily high and that His entire work is to bring about freedom and agency. The fall wasn't some unhappy accident. There has been a world of suffering since then, but Nephi's view restores meaning to life. In this life, God is developing our decision-making skills. He is personally responsible for everything that occurs. He could have removed the tree from Eden with a simple command, but he didn't. Instead, we are free and Nephi shows us God intends to make us "powerful unto deliverance."

The days we live on earth are called "the days of probation" by Nephi, Laman, and Lemuel. We are being tried but **we** are also trying good and evil.

Now, an actual commandment is "love one another." Within the framework we have been discussing, love must therefore be easy and natural at times, but difficult at times as well. Otherwise, we are no freer, and love no more meaningfully, than a greeting card for example. Nephi concludes that men are free to choose "liberty and eternal life" or "captivity and death." He calls the path to agency the "way." I think finally we are truly getting somewhere. If you are reading to this hoping to understand the hype of the Book of Mormon, you can see that some foundations are laid.

Implications of Nephi's Philosophy: Can Only the Educated Truly Sin?

Another implication of Nephi's conception of agency is fundamental to the Nephite perception of reality itself. Wickedness in Nephi's view is the destruction of others' wellbeing, knowledge, agency, happiness, or power. This is not as clear-cut as it may seem at first.

In this life, we all have varying degrees of knowledge and varying abilities to acquire new knowledge. If we know the consequences of our actions, our primary intent does not absolve us from responsibility when we harm others, even if our intentions are good. If people are destroyed as a matter of "collateral damage," that may in fact be as bad as premeditation. After all, we deemed the affected persons to be trivial before we acted. **This is true wickedness:** when we know that our actions will likely destroy others and we persist in those actions.

Such definitions can only be reliably applied by an all-knowing Judge.

Therefore, Nephi writes, "Where there is no law given… the mercies of the Holy One of Israel have claim upon them." He writes, "The atonement satisfieth the demands of his justice upon all those who have not the law given to them … and they are restored to that God who gave them breath which is the Holy One of Israel."

These concepts lead a Nephite prophet to say, "They who have died…in their ignorance, not having salvation declared unto them…have part in the first resurrection, or have eternal life, being redeemed by the Lord."

This seems to be the measuring stick used later by Captain Moroni when he blames the blood of thousands of Nephites on a conniving Nephite ruling class rather than on the Lamanites who are actually doing the killing.

This is echoed by John in the New Testament when he wrote "God sent not his Son into the world to condemn the world but...this is the condemnation, that light is come into the world and men loved darkness rather than light (John 3:16-18)."

Nephi's Philosophy of Hell

Aside from the way to agency, freedom, and eternal life, there is another path. I will now shift our discussion to Nephi's conception of darkness and evil. What did Nephi fight against? What are we fighting against?

A quick look at the ancient conception of Hell will help us appreciate Nephi's beliefs and concepts, and our own as well.

Now, it doesn't matter much whether you end up agreeing with Nephi, or with me. What is important—and above all, useful—is that you look at your beliefs. Ask yourself what you believe, and why. Then, as you are able, go to the primary sources with which **you** are familiar and re-familiarize yourself with each author's intended meaning. Whether there is agreement or disagreement among the concepts you re-encounter, you should end up with an increased degree of self-awareness. Any contrasts between your beliefs and what you get here should make the differences more pronounced and meaningful to you. Alternatively, the story of the blind men and the elephant comes to mind as well. Sometimes we are all describing the same thing without appreciating others' perspectives.

Perhaps it is Nephi's access to a vast amount of literature that makes his writings relevant and worthy of study. To this day many similar themes are found in our media. I've already mentioned Nephi's understanding of "the way." Now, it is time to talk about a river reminiscent to Disney's River Ahtohallan.

Nephi's vision of the tree of life is perhaps the most well-known scripture in the whole Book of Mormon. The fruit of the tree of life and the living waters is, as Nephi says, "the most desirable above all things." I love that the angel giving the vision never told Nephi **what** the fruit was. Instead, he showed Nephi the condescension of God, the birth, and the works of God. Nephi saw God minister to his children and then **Nephi** told the angel what the fruit was. Nephi never had to be told what the fruit was. After he saw and felt the love of God, he knew that **it** was the fruit that is most desirable. How could it be anything else?

As with the fruit, the angel showed to Nephi the meaning of other symbols. Nephi also saw a filthy river. Nephi's father Lehi had the same vision but did not focus on the river and so he did not see its waters in all their filth.

However, Nephi does look into the river, and what he sees leaves him without strength (1 Ne 12:14-19). He writes:

> The angel said unto me: Behold thy seed, and also the seed of thy brethren. And it came to pass that I looked and beheld the people of my seed gathered together in multitudes against the seed of my brethren; and they were gathered together to battle. And the angel spake unto me,

saying: Behold the fountain of filthy water which thy father saw; yea even the river of which he spake; and the depths thereof are the depths of hell…. and **while the angel spake these words, I beheld and saw** that the seed of my brethren did contend against my seed, according to the word of the angel; and because of the pride of my seed, and the temptations of the devil, I beheld that the seed of my brethren did overpower the people of my seed.

Hundreds of thousands were killed in those battles. Each person involved had their own stories to tell. Perhaps Nephi saw some of the scenes Mormon recorded of the dead and dying. Mormon wrote:

For according to the knowledge which I have received from Amoron, behold, the Lamanites have many prisoners, which they took from the tower of Sherrizah; and there were men, women, and children. And the husbands and fathers of those women and children they have slain; and they feed the women upon the flesh of their husbands, and the children upon the flesh of their fathers; and no water, save a little, do they give unto them. And notwithstanding this great abomination of the Lamanites, it doth not exceed that of our people in Moriantum. For behold, many of the daughters of the Lamanites have they taken prisoners; and after depriving them of that which was most dear and precious above all things, which is chastity and virtue— And after they had done this thing, they did murder them in a most cruel manner, torturing their bodies even unto death; and after they have done this, they devour their flesh like unto wild beasts, because of the hardness of their hearts; and they do it for a token of bravery.

Nephi goes on to say that the destruction of his people is his greatest affliction. The pain in his soul nearly consumes him, and it seems he does not talk until he regains his strength. I am not sure how deeply I would

125

look into that river if I were given the chance. But keep in mind, aside from depicting the trials Nephi confronted, this vision explains what hell is.

Now, we tend to think of cultures as largely homogenous groups of people joined by a common set of concepts. In reality, each individual understands a portion of the knowledge available to the culture as a whole. Laman and Lemuel, for example, have an incomplete understanding of hell and ask some important questions about it. For instance, they ask in 1 Nephi 15:31, "Doth this thing mean the torment of the body in the days of probation or doth it mean the final state of the soul after the death of the temporal body, or doth it speak of the things which are temporal?" This may seem like a simple question, but it is a better one than I would have asked in the same situation. I would never have asked if the suffering of hell is associated with the temporal world. I thought everyone knew that it exists apart from this world, on the plane of the afterlife. To my surprise, Nephi responds that the torment of hell is in **both** temporal and spiritual things (vs. 32). This goes along with the depiction of hell seen in the river: something occurring in the physical, tangible world.

What stands out most strikingly to me about Nephi's vision in that river is that people are harming other people. That is the most basic definition of hell I would use. The Nephite concept of hell in a word is helplessness. Unfortunately, in that helplessness one harms others. I don't care where it is. Nephi says that hell can be in either the physical or spiritual world.

To understand the issue better, I studied the use of a Hebrew word, Sheol, which is often translated as "hell" in English. In Proverbs 9:18, we read that the guests of a person of folly are in the depths of hell. Notice the present tense. The verse talks as if the guests of that person are there currently. Additionally, Jonah states that after he was swallowed by the whale, he cried "out of the belly of hell" and God heard him. Perhaps that was an exaggeration; but when was Jonah in hell? How could he have been if he was still living? Was his claim just a poetic turn of phrase?

Altogether, it seems both the Nephites and ancient Israelites use the term hell or Sheol somewhat figuratively, the way we use the term "school." School can refer to any part of life, or to life itself, as in "the school of life." The "school of hard knocks" can represent any period when we learn through difficult experience. Alternatively, other times when we say "school" we mean a very specific place, age group, curriculum, and intensity.

Similarly, hell can be both a specific place and a set of circumstances in which we are separated from the Lord. Thus hell can exist in the premortal life, mortal life, in the spirit world, during the millennium, and after the "last day" or final judgment as well. Likewise, we can be in varying degrees of God's presence at all those times.

We have already talked about God's presence. **There,** we find agency, love, and truth all around us.

Hell is **anything** outside of God's presence. In hell, one lacks knowledge, feels no love, and is captive. In hell, **people** harm each other and are harmed in turn. There, persons are subject to a devil. The term used is "angels to a devil (2 Nephi 9:9)." Now the Book of Mormon records that the redemption of Christ will bring us *back* into the presence of God. And so we learn that we did live before this earth life and that we were good. Indeed, Moroni tells us to be believing as in times of old. Because our nature is inherently good, it would be particularly awful to be a servant of devils. To hurt others is not in our eternal nature. How much worse would we feel if we were made to hurt others against our will and then continue on helplessly doing so? Hell exists even as one hurts others unintentionally. Sadly, hell can be found on earth or after death. When used to describe a specific location, hell is a place where some people reside after death.

I must mention that other prophets one thousand years later in the Book of Mormon seem to distinguish subdivisions of what Nephi termed "hell." Returning to the vision we were discussing, Nephi saw persons who were separate from the tree of life and unable to see God's love due to a mist of darkness. They were therefore in hell. People who cannot see or feel God's love while living on earth are caught in what *other* Nephite prophets appear to term the "gall of bitterness."

As an example, a Nephite prophet patiently explains to his son who genuinely believes all infants who die without baptism may be forever lost and in misery. He explains that those who believe such things are wrapped up by the "gall of bitterness" and separated from God's love. Truly one cannot feel God's love without knowing his immense love for every one of us. Therefore, the only way possible to sincerely believe infants are lost forever is to have one's vision obscured by the mist of darkness.

Another takeaway is that one can be in the gall of bitterness (hell), surrounded by mists of darkness, and not comprehending God's love **without realizing it**. Now, I know that we all have a weakness for binary solutions. To some extent, we like to believe that one is either in hell or not. But many of the principles we have discussed exist on a spectrum and apply "line upon line."

Nephi lumps the gall of bitterness and hell together at times. I mention as an aside that for Nephi, hell seems to be separate from what he calls "the lake of fire." For Nephi "lake of fire" refers to guilt felt upon realization of one's deeds. Later, some Nephite prophets seem to group hell and the lake of fire together. But for Nephi hell is helplessness and involuntary harm.

Here are phrases used by Nephi to characterize hell:

- Hell will be "filled by those who digged it (1 Nephi 14:3)."
- Hell is a "gulf which separates the wicked from the tree of life (love)(1 Nephi 15:26)."
- The wicked "must go down to hell...for...when the Spirit ceaseth to strive with man then cometh speedy destruction (2 Nephi 26:10)."
- Nephi says that hell is associated with ignorance: and is a state of decreased awareness. He writes, the "sleep of hell (2 Nephi 1:13)."

A Nephite prophet wrote (Alma 12:11) to persons "that will harden their hearts, to them is given the lesser portion of the word until they know nothing... Now this is what is meant by the chains of hell."

In hell there is no agency. Nephi wrote, "our spirits must become subject to the devil and we become like unto him (2 Nephi 9:8-12)."

This idea of a spectrum extends beyond the Book of Mormon. Nephi quotes Isaiah to say the devil will "be brought down to hell, to the sides of the pit." "Sides" in this verse יַרְכְּתֵי־ can be understood as "extremities" or "far reaches" or "lowest depths (Isaiah 14:15)."

However, perhaps the more groundbreaking teaching is that hell is temporary. Nephi references:

- "everlasting chains" (2 Nephi 28:19).
- "the eternal gulf of misery and woe" (2 Nephi 1:13).
- "everlasting death" (2 Nephi 10:23).
- "eternal destruction" (2 Nephi 1:22).

As we have discussed, it appears those in the Nephite concept of hell are those who sinned despite knowing better. They knew how to help and how to love, and yet they chose to do the opposite. They cut themselves off from the prosperous presence of the Lord and dwindle.

This is partially reflected in what a Nephite prophet writes "I say unto you that ye would be more miserable to dwell with a holy and just God, under a consciousness of your filthiness before him, than ye would to dwell with the damned souls in hell...When ye shall be brought to see your nakedness before God and also the glory of God and the holiness of Jesus Christ, *it* will kindle a flame of unquenchable fire upon you (Mormon 9:4-5)."

It is no wonder that Nephi writes, "Wo unto the uncircumcised of heart, for a knowledge of their iniquities shall smite them at the last day (2 Nephi 9:33)."

Now it may seem to us that at any time we want we can just decide to be good. I suppose we tell ourselves we know what good is and could do that if we wanted to. But therein is the problem; in hell we do not know what is right. Because of this, we cannot do what is right. We do not know how to help. We have put ourselves in a place of decreased knowledge and awareness. Remember that the chains of hell are ignorance.

Nephi's description of hell reminds me of a more modern example. In *A Christmas Carol,* the Ghost of Christmas Present shows Ebenezer Scrooge a vision of a gaunt, impoverished boy and girl, named Ignorance and Want, respectively. "Beware them both, and all of their degree," says the ghost, "but most of all beware this boy, for on his brow I see that written which is Doom, unless the writing be erased." This is an especially good example of the relationship between ignorance and hell.

And yet, this is where those important proofs of Nephi come in (Nephi writes many things in triplicate with different witnesses in 2 Nephi). Nephi would say that he **proves** we are redeemed from hell. We learn that hell is temporary. He writes, "Hell must deliver up its captive spirits (2 Nephi 9)**." Yet,** he goes on to refer to "**everlasting** chains", "the **eternal** gulf of misery and woe", "**everlasting** death," and "**eternal** destruction." How can this be?

Apparently, this understanding of hell was not widely understood, and Christ spoke to Joseph Smith to clarify.

It is not written that there shall be no end to this torment....

but it is written *endless torment*. Again, it is written *eternal damnation*....

I speak unto you that...you may enter into my rest. Behold... I am endless, and the punishment which is given from my hand is endless punishment, for Endless is my name. Wherefore—

Eternal punishment is God's punishment.

Endless punishment is God's punishment.

Therefore I command you to repent—repent, lest I smite you by the rod of my mouth, and by my wrath, and by my anger, and your sufferings be sore—how sore you know not, how exquisite you know not, yea, how hard to bear you know not.

For behold, I, God, have suffered these things for all, that they might not suffer if they would repent; But if they would not repent they must suffer even as I;

Which suffering caused myself, even God, the greatest of all, to tremble because of pain, and to bleed at every pore, and to suffer both body and spirit—and would that I might not drink the bitter cup, and shrink…

Wherefore, I command you again to repent, lest I humble you with my almighty power…lest you suffer these punishments of which I have spoken, of which in the smallest, yea, even in the least degree you have tasted at the time I withdrew my Spirit (Doctrine & Covenants 19:6 – 20).

Nephi's writings are consistent. If the Lord merely withdraws his spirit, a host of forces can have their way with us. Without knowledge, we and whatever we protect are reduced to prey. At the end of the passage we just read, we again saw the concept "degree." Certainly, as valuable as God's children are to him, He only withdraws from us to the extent that is helpful. There is no reason for us to be cut off forever.

Nephi tells us that despite the anguish of his soul over the slain of his people, he admits that God is just. While the Lord's punishment may be less than we deserve, it is never more than is just. God always dispenses punishment with purpose. It is no wonder that Nephi rejoices in the eventual miraculous redemption of his people.

We've discussed Nephi's writings and his philosophy. I find his writings daunting and simultaneously energizing and empowering. With a greater appreciation of these things, let's return to the question of his personality and character.

Chapter 3

Nephi's Character

Nephi's Strengths

Leadership
Malleable, open-minded, listens
Innovative (makes: tools, bow, swords, ocean-worthy boat, buildings)
Seasoned teacher
Successful in any endeavour
Physical strength, warrior
Resilience (attitude)
Visionary

Unsurprisingly, Nephi seems to excel at **leadership.** After all, he lived for at least eight years among people who wanted to kill him. He writes that his company was "led with one accord" to the Promised Land. So it seems that he was able at times to get Laman and Lemuel to agree on a common vision. We also read that his people looked upon him as a king.

Nephi appears to be a **flexible leader and is someone who listens.** Nephi was willing to consider his father's suggestions and copiously records his brother's concerns, showing a good and balanced understanding of other people's opinions.

Nephi is a **teacher.** He teaches a whole society many useful skills; Jacob seems to be his protégé.

Nephi also has great **strength**. Nephi mentions restraining Zoram. Additionally, he is a warrior. Jacob says that Nephi "wielded the sword of Laban in their defense."

Nephi demonstrates **resilience and perseverance**. The best example of Nephi's resilience is that we have no record of him complaining or murmuring even when starvation seemed inevitable.

Nephi was a **visionary**. Far from merely reacting to events, Nephi had long-term goals. Taken at face value, "long-term" is an understatement: Nephi set goals that would be accomplished approximately two to three thousand years in the future.

Nephi's Weaknesses

Perhaps too open and forthright	Alma 45:9
"Anger"	2 Ne 4:27
Complacency in wilderness?	Alma 37:38-41
Strength slackens	2 Ne 4:26

Moving on to weaknesses. As we mentioned early on, Nephi's writings tend not to be very personal, which makes it difficult to learn much about his personality.

I will address Nephi's perspectives on race and pride in a separate section. As to the rest of his weak spots, here is what I have come up with.

Nephi may have been **too frank.** He seemed to share a lot. Nephi claims to have written many of his texts for his people, in some cases exclusively for them. He accepts as a matter of fact that all Nephites will become extinct about 400 years after the coming of Christ. It must not have been easy to build a society knowing it was doomed, and it certainly wasn't easy for the Nephites to read that fact stated so plainly. Centuries later, Alma instructs his son **not** to share his knowledge of the Nephites' pending extinction. At the same time, Nephi's openness might have helped the Nephites live as long as they did. His openness, then, could be seen as a strength, albeit one that sometimes put people back on their heels.

Nephi mentions that he is **angry** on one occasion and characterizes this as a weakness. He writes in 2 Nephi 4 that he is angry because of his enemies. But why is Nephi angry? In 1 Nephi, he was bound for days, beaten, and left for dead. Through that entire ordeal, he only mentions being **"grieved."** Now, in 2 Nephi, he writes that he is angry. What in the world could make Nephi angry? In the very next chapter, Nephi writes, "it sufficeth me to say that forty years had passed away and we had already had wars and contentions with our brethren."

Nephi is a leader, seen as a king. He even designs and produces weapons. In any war, he and his family would be high-value military targets. His anger may have its roots in the desperation he felt during this time.

We can't know precisely what Nephi was angry about, or what made his "heart weep" or what made his "soul linger in the valley of sorrow." But each of us can look to our own lives for examples of how anger can take hold when we deal with difficult situations over long periods.

Nephi also tells us that **his strength slackens**, which we might take as a sign of **complacency.** Complacency is the opposite of resilience. Years later, a Nephite descendant states that their fathers were slothful while looking at the Liahona compass because of the "easiness of the way." It is not clear that this slacking-off applied to Nephi in particular, or if it was meant to describe the group as a whole.

Throughout his writings, we see Nephi grow. Some commentators have pointed out that Nephi had an abundance of **zeal** that he had to temper. This is based on the observation that Nephi seems to qualify some of his early statements. This is certainly plausible, as the dangers of being overly zealous are discussed several times among the Nephites.

Contemporary Criticisms

Manipulative	1 Ne 16:28, Alma 54:23
Usurper	1 Ne 16:26, Mosiah 10:15
Liar (about revelations)	1 Ne 16:28
Uses "cunning arts"	1 Ne 16:28
Dreamer	1 Ne 17:20
Judgemental	1 Ne 17:22
Stole brass plates from **Laman**	Mosiah 10:16
Delusions of Grandeur	1 Ne 17:17,19

Now, what do Nephi's contemporaries say of him? Laman and Lemuel have incentive to find fault with Nephi. And a lot of the criticism they give is the same that all leaders must face. They depict him as manipulative. A usurper, a liar, a dreamer, judgmental. A thief and a person with cunning arts who has delusions of grandeur. Most of us have at one time thought of a boss, a politician, or a parent in some of these terms.

Some of these criticisms may be due to Nephi's role as a leader and would likely have been attributed to whoever was in charge. But this does offer us a different perspective on Nephi. Let's look at two of the more unique charges: that he was judgmental, and that he used cunning arts to maintain power.

His contemporaries said that Nephi was like his father, who had judged the people of Jerusalem. According to this perspective, the people of Jerusalem were good. Remember, there doesn't seem to be any desperation in Jerusalem at the time of Nephi's departure. The destruction of Jerusalem isn't confirmed to the Nephites until the appearance of Mulek's descendants hundreds of years later (Helaman 8:21). So eventually, even persons not informed through divine revelation eventually knew that Jerusalem was destroyed. At the time Laman and Lemuel likely had no way to confirm it.

The criticism of **cunning arts** is the most pointed one on our list. "Cunning" is always used negatively in the Book of Mormon. People accused of being cunning include deceitful and disingenuous kings, evil lawyers, charismatic dissidents, flatterers, and others of that ilk. This doesn't seem to be some way you would describe, say, an awkward fool. Cunning implies deliberate manipulation. It amounts to an accusation that Nephi governed his people in bad faith.

Specifically, Laman and Lemuel say "he worketh many things by his cunning arts, that he may deceive." This could refer to the time Nephi physically shocked Laman and Lemuel as a sign that God was with him, or perhaps they think that Nephi somehow fabricated the Liahona compass. Alternatively, Laman and Lemuel could be referring to Nephi's language. I only know of a few of the literary tools Nephi used. Additionally, we only have Nephi's writings and Nephi says his oral skills were much superior. Enough, perhaps, to be labeled "cunning."

Is Nephi's literary skill a cunning art?

If Nephi were alive today, perhaps we would think of him as a poet or a lyricist. Even in translation, some catchy one-liners come through: "Adam fell that men might be. Men are that they might have joy."

At least one well-documented technique Nephi used is the chiasmus. Chiasmus is a Greek word that means "cross." A chiasmus repeats your ideas in reverse order. For example, a well-known chiasmus in English is John F. Kennedy's "Ask not what your country can do for you but ask what you can do for your country."

Let's take a look at Nephi's narration of the death of Laban. We could call this text a "homicide chiasmus."

Short chiasmus can exist in every language intentionally and by sheer chance as well. There are other chiasmus that are much longer. The odds of putting words together and getting a chiasmus of say six lines are probably similar to the odds of randomly writing six letters and hoping for a word. It is not impossible; it will happen occasionally.

Because there are hundreds of chiasmus in the Book of Mormon, some people argue the Book of Mormon was written by someone with extensive or even native knowledge of Hebrew. Some state this is evidence of authenticity as the concept of chiasmus was largely unknown in the 1800s. Consequently, others are quick to discredit the presence of chiasmus in the Book of Mormon. I am going to treat that issue as a distraction.

But, as a self-indulging side, I noticed when I lived in Guatemala there was tension between Guatemalans with western lifestyles and those with indigenous lifestyles. And of course, there were people in the middle who incorporated portions of both lifestyles. Among the Mayan writings is a book called the *Popol Vuh*, which has recorded a devastating flood that destroyed the world. This and other parts sound similar to the biblical account of Genesis. A person sympathetic to the indigenous might mention the flood as evidence that the ancient Mayans were inspired and had revelations on par with all prophets of old. That is to say, the Mayans were divinely inspired, and God talked to them. Alternatively, people wanting to discredit that point would at times say that the Mayans had to write their history according to what the Spanish would accept. This would subtly discredit the fidelity of extant Mayan writings and simultaneously point out their subjugate state.

Chiasmus in Mayan Texts

Of the thirty-seven Mayan documents I examined, chiastic patterns abound in sixteen. I discovered that the texts with chiasms had several traits in common: They had early sixteenth-century dates of composition, authorship by royal family members, internal evidence of reliance on pre-Columbian hieroglyphic books, significant references to Mayan history and religion, and relative freedom from European words and cultural influences.

None of the highland Mayan documents composed after 1580 include passages of chiasmus. By that time, the people familiar with ancient hieroglyphic books were, for the most part, gone.

Chiasmus in Mayan Texts (Christenson, 1988)

However, I was happy to find an article written by a scholar who compares writings from the first generation of conquered Mayans; those who spoke Maya and the writings of the second generation of conquered Mayans who were allowed to speak Spanish only. Chiasmus were found in the writings of the first generation only. I find this validates the content of writings such as the *Popol Vuh* and suggests there was less Spanish influence than otherwise presumed.

Returning to the Book of Mormon, some statistical models can predict the intentionality of a chiasmus. However, these tools and their validation are beyond me. I would rather put effort into other areas. If I am worried about the randomness or intentionality of a chiasmus, I try to interpret the text in both ways. If the text is a chiasmus the "main point" is supposedly in the very middle. Regardless, I ask myself, what is the author really trying to say?

That brings us to an apparent chiasmus that narrates the slaying of Laban. Now, homicides tend to be very messy affairs. Nephi's narration of Laban's killing seems to:

- create order in the narration
- propel logic and persuasiveness
- help the reader process the narrative
- reinforce memory
- justify the slaying

Nephi in Disguise Obtaining the Brass Plates

Here is the narrative, in a series of excerpts from the account in 1 Nephi 4.

And it was by night; and I caused that [my brothers] should hide themselves without the walls. And after they had hid themselves, I, Nephi, crept into the city and went forth towards the house of Laban.

And I was led by the Spirit, not knowing beforehand the things which I should do.

Nevertheless I went forth, and as I came near unto the house of Laban I beheld a man, and he had fallen to the earth before me, for he was drunken with wine.

And when I came to him I found that it was Laban.

And I beheld his sword, and I drew it forth from the sheath thereof; and the hilt thereof was of pure gold, and the workmanship thereof was exceedingly fine, and I saw that the blade thereof was of the most precious steel.

And it came to pass that I was constrained by the Spirit that I should kill Laban; but I said in my heart: Never at any time have I shed the blood of man. And I shrunk and would that I might not slay him.

And the Spirit said unto me again: Behold the Lord hath delivered him into thy hands. Yea, and I also knew that he had sought to take away mine own life; yea, and he would not hearken unto the commandments of the Lord; and he also had taken away our property.

And it came to pass that the Spirit said unto me again: Slay him, for the Lord hath delivered him into thy hands;

Behold the Lord slayeth the wicked to bring forth his righteous purposes. It is better that one man should perish than that a nation should dwindle and perish in unbelief.

And now, when I, Nephi, had heard these words, I remembered the words of the Lord which he spake unto me in the wilderness, saying that: Inasmuch as thy seed shall keep my commandments, they shall prosper in the land of promise.

Yea, and I also thought that they could not keep the commandments of the Lord according to the law of Moses, save they should have the law.

And I also knew that the law was engraven upon the plates of brass.

And again, I knew that the Lord had delivered Laban into my hands for this cause -- that I might obtain the records according to his commandments.

Therefore I did obey the voice of the Spirit, and took Laban by the hair of the head, and I smote off his head with his own sword.

And after I had smitten off his head with his own sword, I took the garments of Laban and put them upon mine own body; yea, even every whit; and I did gird on his armor about my loins.

And after I had done this, I went forth unto the treasury of Laban.

And Zoram did follow me, as I went forth...without the walls.

A My brethren did follow me up until we came **without the walls of Jerusalem.**

    B I went **forth towards the house of Laban** not knowing beforehand the things I should do.

        C **I beheld his sword**, the hilt was of pure gold...and I saw that the blade thereof was of the most precious steel.

            D I was **constrained by the Spirit** that I should kill Laban but I said in my heart: Never at any time have I shed the blood of man. And I shrunk and would that I might not slay him.

                E And the Spirit said unto me again: **Behold the Lord hath delivered him into thy hands.** Yea, and I also knew that he had sought to take away mine own life; and he also had taken away our property.

                    F I remembered the words of the Lord... "Inasmuch as thy seed shall **keep my commandments** they shall prosper in the land."

                    F' I also thought they could not **keep the commandments** save they should have the law and I also knew that the law was engraven upon the plates of brass.

                E' And again, I knew that **the Lord had delivered Laban into my hands**... that I might obtain the records according to His commandments.

            D' Therefore I did **obey the voice of the Spirit** and took Laban and I smote off his head.

        C' **With his own sword...**

    B' I... **went forth unto the treasury of Laban.**

A' **Zoram did follow me,** as I went forth **without the walls.**

Chiasmus in 1 Nephi 4

When one looks at this narration, it seems to entail a legal justification for Laban's murder. That fact changes how you understand it. Nephi states that he went "not knowing beforehand the things [he] should do." Some people take this as an assertion that failing to plan is somehow the same as moving in faith, or that if you have faith, you can go without a plan!

📖   Numbers 35

20 But if he "thrust him of hatred, or hurl at him by laying of wait, that he die;

21 Or in enmity smite him with his hand, that he die: he that smote *him* shall surely be put to death; *for* he *is* a murderer:

Numbers 35:20-21 KJV

That may be true at times, but I don't think that is Nephi's point here, and he certainly doesn't make that argument anywhere else that I can find. In Numbers 35:20, the law of Moses states if a person dies by one laying in wait, then it is murder. Nephi may be confirming as part of his defense that he goes to Laban without the intention to harm.

Later in this narration, it seems odd that Nephi goes into such detail about the metal used to make his sword. Nephi wrote the "blade thereof was of the most precious steel." Again, in Numbers, by law, if iron is used in a death, it is murder.

Now, steel is simply iron that has been infused with carbon. Low-quality steel would be regarded by people of Nephi's time as, well, iron. Nephi happens to include the detail that the sword is the "most precious steel."

145

16 And if he smite him with an instrument of iron, so that he die, he *is* a murderer

Numbers 35:16 KJV

Additionally, in the full account, Nephi leaves out the name of the servant of Laban until the end, perhaps to keep readers from suspecting a conspiracy.

Aside from legal justification, Nephi has good reason to encourage people to process the incident with Laban. Remember, Nephi will found an entire society, and he can hardly allow murder to be easily justified.

The center of the chiasmus—the pivot of the narration—is often considered its main point. Looking at other homicide narrations in the Bible, the narrative center also may reflect special circumstances to take into consideration. The center of this chiasmus concerns **keeping the commandments.**

Now, obviously, I didn't know about any of this as a young child, but I do remember reading this story of Laban. I felt how very important the brass plates and God's commandments were. Somehow, Nephi has turned the story of Laban's killing into a lesson on keeping the commandments. This puts Laban's slaying on the back burner, diminishing its importance and impact.

It appears this strategy was effective. For the next hundreds of years, people regularly criticized Nephi, and yet I don't see that anyone ever accused him of murder. In fact, the only time the plates seem to come up is when the Lamanites allege Nephi wrongfully took the plates from Laman, his older brother. To shift the narration so effectively for the next hundred years is truly a remarkable feat.

And, as for the sword of Laban, far from being stigmatized or hidden as a murder weapon, it is passed down and used by the Nephite kings, seemingly it stands as a symbol of divine investiture. The sword is also one of few relics buried years later with the plates of gold. Even today, among Latter-day Saints the sword of Laban is generally regarded as an important relic, not as a murder weapon.

If the slaying of Laban had been narrated differently, would it have been perceived differently? Would we think of it differently? Perhaps this is one of the "cunning arts" that Laman and Lemuel ruminated on.

Going even further, it is reasonable to wonder whether Nephi studied law before he fled Jerusalem. That is certainly possible, but Nephi didn't write this account until thirty years later. He had time to process his story and consult with others. I doubt that only a lawyer could write this. So, while this account suggests knowledge of Israelite law, Nephi's vocational training remains a mystery (additional discussion in appendix 2).

If this is all true, why did God let it happen? Couldn't God have found another way, like putting Laban into a prolonged sleep? If God wanted Laban dead, couldn't he simply have made it happen? Why make Nephi do this? I don't know the answer to that. However, I do think it is worth noting other people who Nephi may have killed. I mentioned that Nephi writes of many wars with his brethren. Nephi had either to deal with these situations himself or to help others negotiate them. It seems Nephi was being prepared to be "mighty even unto the power of deliverance," as he says.

Chapter 4

Nephi's Literary Goals and Worldview

Nephi's Literary Goals

Whatever his technique, and however "cunning" people may have found it, I do think that Nephi is an effective writer. While I don't know all the literary techniques at play, I know that most books don't cause millions of people to mobilize or relocate.

Now, Nephi claims at least three purposes for his writing. **First,** to persuade people to come to God. **Second,** to show us that God will make us mighty and deliver us. And **third,** that whosoever reads his words will rejoice.

On a personal note, I can say that as I have read and studied Nephi's words, I do rejoice. I feel invigorated with life. I consider myself a skeptic. Yet, I have become more optimistic about the future despite the devastatingly bad news we seem to hear every day. I genuinely believe that good will prevail, and yet I feel that sense of optimism to be a reason for greater motivation, not for complacency. I have also become more enthusiastic about the Bible. While researching, I came across a list that categorized Ezekiel as a minor prophet. While I knew that that was a mistake, the strength of my reaction surprised me. It felt like a gut punch. I never would have responded that way previously. To me, Ezekiel became more than just another scripture character. He became a real person who, like Nephi, leaves Jerusalem and never stops talking about it.

It is also worth pointing out that Mormon says after searching the Nephite records that Nephi's writings were pleasing and choice to him. Mormon is someone that witnessed first-hand the destruction of his people. I imagine it would take a lot to reassure anyone who has lost so much.

Altogether, I believe that scripture including Nephi's words is like a compass: by looking at them daily, one can find direction, strength, knowledge, courage, stamina, and hope. By frequent small corrections, we are led to the Promised Lands.

One can test this view by assessing an ability as they see fit at baseline and after a month of reading perhaps ten minutes of Nephi's writings daily. Again, a simple experiment, but one that should isolate the effect of Nephi's words on an individual reader. Such an experiment is important. After all, Ezekiel states that we shall know what the Lord has performed and spoken **after** He places his spirit in us (Ezekiel 37:14).

Nephi is a person who wrote throughout a long career and had records from times that included the height of Jerusalem's power. He seems to use every bit of knowledge and experience at his disposal for his purposes. For us that is helpful, but for his brothers, it may have been polarizing. With this knowledge, it seems Nephi likely has an anecdote or a historical tale for every situation. I imagine that this helped some family but annoyed others.

Speaking of double-edge swords, there is some downside to Nephi's notoriety.

Nephi Sensationalized

There is evidence that Nephi and his works were at times sensationalized. Examples of this include:

- A later prophet romanticizes Nephi's time, wishing he lived in that day.

- Laman and Lemuel worship Nephi on one occasion, and he must correct them.

- After joining with the Mulekites, only descendants of Nephi are allowed to be king (Mosiah 25:13). This likely led to an unfortunate class system based on ancestry. To be fair, the Mulekites were initially illiterate, and the tradition is later abolished.

- For unclear reasons, Jacob claims the designation "the Brother of Nephi" twice in his records.

- As a leader, Nephi seems to attempt to distance himself from the role of advice-giver or oracle. Perhaps he is asked too regularly for advice. Nephi states that he is grieved that he must instruct people what to do. He exhorts his people to follow their own personal revelations from the Holy Ghost, scriptures, and prayer (2 Nephi 32).

- At one point, there is a plan to call all future kings "Nephi." They will be called First Nephi, Second Nephi, and so on. Perhaps this was in the spirit of "first captain", "second captain," and so on, as we mentioned earlier.

How Pride and Racism Interact

With so many people wishing to lionize him, Nephi needed to guard himself and his people against the dangers of pride. As it turns out, pride is a persistent theme in his life and writing.

The Lord states, "Beware of pride lest ye become as the Nephites of old (Doctrine & Covenants 38:39)." Nephi writes he saw his children were destroyed because of their pride and temptations. Mormon writes, "The pride of this nation...hath proven their destruction (Moroni 8:27)." It may be impossible to talk about the Nephites without talking about pride.

Indeed, it seems the people of Nephi had a propensity to esteem themselves very highly. I just noted that for some time, only descendants of Nephi could be king. Also, Jacob writes that Nephites thought themselves better than their neighbors when they were more successful in finding gold. Furthermore, Jacob tells the Nephites to "revile no more against [the Lamanites] because of the darkness of their skins." Unfortunately, substantial evidence exists that Nephites treated women as property. A concise video essay on the subject can be found by searching "Women in the Book of Mormon" on YouTube. Now, I don't want to make this personal, but if you are a Gentile in the last days, it seems the Nephites also thought they were more righteous than you! Nephi writes that he wishes his people would "not suppose they are more righteous" than the latter-day Gentiles.

Because of such pride some leaders felt it necessary to counter the prevailing tenets among the Nephites with provocative examples to the contrary. Later kings and prophets worked in the fields and refused support from their servants. They taught through their actions that all persons are equal.

It seems that pride is a universal sin, as Joseph Smith had to curb its influences as well. At times, Joseph met emigrants arriving in Nauvoo dressed in the worst clothes he could find. He told them that if they expected him to be anything other than a man, they might as well get right back on the boat and go back to England. That sort of welcome would surely have been memorable.

That seems to be a start at defining the problem of pride, and how it can affect entire cultures. When that happens, racism often follows—as surely in Nephi's day as in ours.

Nephi and Race

Now, one of the most controversial aspects of Nephi's writing is the way he handles race. Many people cite portions of Nephi's writing while raising concerns over racial equity. People can read Nephi carefully and genuinely view him as biased or racist. At the same time, leaders of the Church of Jesus Christ of Latter-day Saints frequently cite Nephi to demonstrate that God sees all persons equally. In fact, some of the most explicitly equitable passages in any book of scripture are found in Nephi's writings (2 Nephi 26:33).

Personally, I would say that Nephi is progressive for his day. We find in Nephi's writings that God calls prophets among all peoples. Nephi also states that the Jews of his time were no more favored by the Lord than heathens unless they were righteous. Would many Jews state that they share equal footing in the eyes of God with non-Abrahamic peoples (1 Nephi 17:34)? It appears that Nephi's views on race and tradition are complex.

So, what is going on here? I'll do my best not to approach this as an apologist, although a bit of bias is probably unavoidable for me. I would like to know if Nephi was racist or not in order to get a full and balanced opinion of his character. What is going on? What challenges did he face, and what solutions did he come up with?

As we get into this controversial subject, I should add that I would not judge anyone for maintaining a negative opinion on Nephi's outlook or any of these topics. I believe that if a particular issue is not found offensive today, it is only a matter of time before an offensive topic will come up. Indeed, I have stated that the gospel is intentionally built with room for various interpretations, as a way to preserve agency. The gospel must be easy at times, and it must also be difficult at times.

I should also point out that many Latter-day Saints deem it taboo to look at the prophets as human. I recently heard a Latter-day Saint film director say that the prophets tell us they are not perfect, but **we** don't believe them.

As I have learned to see Nephi and all church members as human, my appreciation for God's plan deepened. This perspective allows me to look more critically at the scriptures and understand them better.

So I don't mind looking at Nephi through a critical and even a skeptical lens.

At times, Nephi describes his people and the Gentiles both as white, fair, and beautiful. It seems like Nephi is inadvertently saying that people with white skin are inherently more beautiful. Later, he also states that the Lamanites are not enticing to his people, as they have a skin of blackness placed on them. Furthermore, although the Lamanites are more righteous in the end, throughout most of the text they are portrayed as the villains, as a marked and cursed people. I suppose it is ironic that the book claims Lamanites as its target audience.

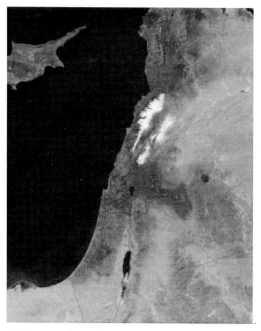

Lebanon and Israel, NASA images (Public Domain)

So what is going on? It certainly appears that Nephi is speaking to us from a white-centric view.

It has been demonstrated that "white" in Hebrew is often synonymous with righteousness, purity, or cleanliness. You will recognize the root of the Hebrew word for "white" — "L-B-N" — in the word "Lebanon." Satellite images show us that the place in Israel's immediate neighborhood where one might have seen snow is right there in Lebanon. Lebanon has mountains that are closer to heaven than anything nearby. The tops of those mountains are white with snow throughout the winter and into the spring. How could one not associate white with heaven?

Other words in Hebrew that share this root include those denoting **the moon** and **frankincense.** The life-saving manna that miraculously appeared and saved the Israelites in the wilderness was white. White is associated with repentance, cleaning, abundance, and a loved woman.

Additionally, in a study published by Carlos Carretero at the Israel Institute of Biblical Studies it is noted that white is often used to celebrate military victories. Perhaps it is white's association with heaven that caused leaders of the ancient world to try to associate themselves with white and therefore deity.

All of these associations—the moon, snow, mountains, heaven, and military power—were consciously and subconsciously present when the term was used in ancient times. Which of those things, if any, did Nephi mean when he used the word? I think he probably meant a combination of all of them. Indeed, just before and after mentioning the whiteness of the Gentiles, Nephi mentions that God supports them militarily. The Gentiles are brought out of captivity and then are successful in battle (1 Nephi 13).

To be clear, we all have cultural biases. For example, why does a bride traditionally wear white to her wedding in our society? Nephi certainly wasn't immune to those cultural influences. The important questions revolve around what Nephi did with the time and choices given to him. My position is that Nephi most likely used these cultural phenomena in wartime to preserve his people.

Let's look ahead a few years and talk about Nephi's nephew, Enos. He hunts; we are told that hunting is a common Lamanite activity. Enos writes that he reflects on the joy of the saints he hears about. By implication, he seems to count himself outside their number. He also prays for the Lamanites and writes that he spends his time among them.

Enos also writes the first first-person book I can find in a period of more than four hundred years that doesn't begin with a self-written declaration in the third person. This is a deliberate change in tradition or at least a lessened concern for Israelite tradition. Aside from all that, Enos is presumably one of the most reliable persons among the Nephites, as he was trusted with the record left by Nephi and Jacob. To be clear, I am not saying anything negative about Enos. He may have achieved a perfect balance.

My point is that Enos's pursuit of traditionally Lamanite activities, his abandonment of literary traditions, his minimal journal entries, and others' future excuses such as the lack of metal to write with, suggest that it may have been hard to convince the Nephite youth to be Nephites in the established tradition of the time. Consider that metalworking was one of the chief things Nephi states he taught his people about. And yet, in a few years, they will explain there are few metal plates. At the end of the day, Nephi writes that he caused his people to be industrious. Between that work and the study of learning the eight hundred or so Egyptian glyphs, as well as the paleo-

Hebrew characters, preserving tradition may not have seemed to be a desirable or immediately useful lifestyle. This is especially true as Egypt and Israel were thousands of miles away. We do read that the Nephites in general did retain literacy, however, it appears Laman and Lemuel did not prioritize literacy since their descendants needed to be taught to keep records, "that they might write one to another (Mosiah 24:6)."

In short, it seems that the Lamanite lifestyle appeared more enticing. To me, this is the problem Nephi is facing. And Nephi states specifically that skin color was used to make the Lamanites less enticing to his people. Far from being ignorant of the cultural phenomena, Nephi is educated, likely aware, and tries to use it as an advantage. Nephi says the Lord "will cause [the Lamanites to] be loathsome unto [his] people." Was this something that Nephi requested of the Lord? Indeed, the Lamanites complained hundreds of years later and said, "The Lord heard [Nephi's] prayers and answered them (Mosiah 10:13)."

It may seem telling that the Nephites could be swayed in this manner. The fact of the matter is that because of their then-present cultural biases, dark skin was unappealing to them to the point that it could be exploited to change behavior.

Aside from the distractions of Lamanite life, the Nephites were in a time of war (2 Nephi 5:34). This would have been a contributing factor.

As we mentioned earlier, Nephi is well educated. He had to know that calling attention to their darker skin would stigmatize and isolate the Lamanites in the eyes of the

Nephites. Indeed, according to Nephi himself, this was the very purpose of focusing on their skin tone.

In my opinion, there absolutely was racism and classism among the people of Nephi. If this is still a question, Jacob, the brother of Nephi tells his people "to revile no more against them because of the darkness of their skins." In fact, pride is exactly the issue that most prophets preach about. The prophets write about times of righteousness in the Book of Mormon in terms of equality, sharing, and love. When a decline into wickedness begins, the Book of Mormon indicates the slide by highlighting inequality or states that the people "began to be divided into classes (4 Nephi 1:26)." And, spoiler alert, all the Nephites die. This destruction occurs explicitly because they consider themselves better than others.

So, it does seem that skin color was used to marginalize people. Unfortunately, gender, wealth, and ancestry also appear to be used by Nephites as wedge issues. It is no wonder that Enos's son Jarom commented that the Lord "has not as yet swept [the Nephites] off from the face of the land." Regardless, about 100 years later after that, the Nephites would have to flee and relocate again, presumably because the Lord would not support the main group of Nephites.

In reality, the message of the Book of Mormon is this: pride exists and pride will get you killed. It doesn't matter who you are or who you were. I don't care what one's pride is based on. To be clear, there can be a righteous type of pride, such as healthy pride in a job well done. The pride I am referring to here is the belief that one is better than another person.

Unfortunately, this exact message is desperately needed in our day. How many cultures out there place a higher value on lighter-toned individuals? Any is too many.

Some may say this is unfair. Why should an attitude or belief merit getting one killed? Nephi clarifies this. He writes about why God destroys the wicked. He writes, "for He will not suffer that the wicked shall destroy the righteous. Wherefore he will preserve the righteous by his power even if it so be that the fulness of his wrath must come (1 Nephi 22:16-17)."

In my opinion, pride is such an awful sin because it inevitably leads to harming others. Harming others is what God cares about. Riddle me this: If you consider all persons to be of equal value to yourself, what sins or harms would you commit against anyone? I haven't thought of one yet.

We live in a world where some seniors think they are better than freshmen, some administrators think they are better than employees. Not just more accomplished and more experienced, but fundamentally better, and for reasons that will naturally and inevitably change over time. What if I were to ask you whether I am better than my neighbor? Since you don't know anything about me, I presume you would say of course not. What if I was a CEO? Now am I better than my neighbor? What would it take for you to say I was better than my neighbor? What would it take for you to say you are better than your neighbor? This comes down to the problem of pride. In reality, we often do think that we know better than others, or that we are fundamentally better than others. The Nephites seemed to be the very embodiment of this destructive pride. Which is pride that leads to harming others. That is what God does not tolerate.

Before considering Nephi's approach to this problem, I should point out that Nephi generally ignores all other races in his prophecy. Why is that?

For starters, we read in 3 Nephi 10:16 that prophets generally speak only to their offspring. Additionally, by extending his message beyond his people, Nephi would risk competing with or even overshadowing prophets who belonged to other peoples. The Lord has a more reasonable plan than that. Nephi reminds us that God speaks "unto all nations of the earth …" and that "the Nephites and the Jews shall have the words of the lost tribes of Israel, and the lost tribes of Israel shall have the words of the Nephites and the Jews (2 Nephi 29:12-13)." Nephi believes that all peoples have prophets and other inspired figures. If we believe Nephi, we must then believe that there are prophets and prophetesses among our ancestry and that other books and records will come forth. After all, "great are the promises of the Lord unto them who are upon the isles of the sea; wherefore as it says isles, there must needs be more than this (2 Nephi 10:21)."

Nephi's Solution to Pride and Racism

So, what is Nephi's approach to the linked problems of pride and racism? Remember, he has seen the fall of his people, and he knows that this happens because of **pride.** Nephi writes about the destruction of three white things in his books.

He writes that the Gentiles were "white, and exceedingly fair and beautiful, like unto **my people** before they were slain (1 Nephi 13:15)." The juxtaposition of the term white and slain must have been striking. Remember, this is a prophecy: Nephi is telling his people that their children will eventually be slain.

Next are the Gentiles. Nephi writes, "Wo be unto the Gentiles, saith the Lord God of Hosts! For notwithstanding I shall lengthen out mine arm unto them from day to day, **they will deny me**; nevertheless, I will be merciful unto them, saith the Lord God, if they will repent and come unto me; for mine arm is lengthened out all the day long." At first, Nephi's words must have been deeply striking—they seem to imply that the Gentiles are **completely** destroyed. Nephi clarifies, "Because of the words which have been spoken ye need not suppose that the Gentiles are *utterly* destroyed." Nephi has over-emphasized the destruction of the Gentiles and now he must walk it back.

Prior to this, Nephi had said that the Gentiles had been humble, and even had the power of God resting on them. Despite that and their whiteness, it is assured they will be destroyed if they deviate from continued righteousness. That brings us to the third white thing that Nephi says is destroyed. On this occasion, he destroys it himself.

Laban. Scholars agree that "Laban" means white. Now, there is much we still do not know about ancient Hebrew vowels. Perhaps Nephi could emphasize various aspects of the word with a change in intonation or emphasis. There could certainly be layers of meaning that we don't grasp. But why does Nephi tell the story of Laban in the first place? Is he writing a sort of explanation out of worry that readers might believe that he is a murderer? Or is Nephi using the story as evidence of divine endorsement? Is Nephi trying to demonstrate an example of perseverance and righteousness? Those are possible interesting interpretations. But I think there is another option.

In the story, Nephi goes up to get the plates from Mr. White, or "Laban" as he was called. To the average Israelite, white connoted the divine, purity, and cleanliness. Now, who was Laban supposed to be? Laban was the guardian of the brass plates. He came from a long line of diligent parents who kept the record intact for generations. Laban was trusted and viewed as an elder in Israel. Laban was endowed with everything he needed to build and fortify Jerusalem, not weaken it. Today we would refer to him as the "old guard," or at least he should've been part of the old guard. Laban should have preserved Jerusalem's strength, and not been reduced to murdering adolescents for wares or asking the wrong questions.

Both Isaiah and Nephi undoubtedly had Laban's persona in mind when they wrote, "the ancient, he is the head and the prophet that teacheth lies, he is the tail. For the leaders of this people cause them to err." The Lord inquires of these ancient elders of Israel, "What mean ye? Ye beat my people to pieces and **grind** the faces of the poor."

Nephi's slaying of Laban can be viewed as symbolic. Keep in mind, we read that Laban could command fifty persons. Indeed, Nephi writes "The Lord will replace the mighty man...the prudent... and the ancient; the captain of fifty... and .... give children to be [Israel's] princes. And babes shall rule over them (Isaiah 3:2-4)."

Laban was at one time the confidant of the Jewish elders, a mighty and powerful man. He was rich and had every opportunity for education and wisdom. When Nephi takes the sword of Laban, he is taking the equivalent of the sword of divinity. When Nephi slays Laban he does so with the sword of purity. Then Nephi puts on the clothes of Laban. But Nephi doesn't use the word **clothes**. He uses the term "garment" which seems to be used in the Book of Mormon to emphasize spiritual standing. Nephi wrote, "I took the garments of Laban and put them upon mine own body; **yea, even every whit;** and I did gird on his armor about my loins."

Nephi took much more than Laban's head and clothes that day. The mantle of guiding and caring for Israel to his best ability then rested on his shoulders. A child had to grow up. Nephi is the person Laban was meant to be: a guide, a leader, and a teacher.

Nephi says of Laban or Mr. White, "Behold the Lord slayeth the wicked to bring forth his righteous purposes."

Nephi tells his people this. Unfortunately for Nephi, the pattern does not stop with Laban. The Nephites at times are good, commune with God, and are blessed by God in battle. They prosper and they are happy. Despite this, they turn away from righteousness to wickedness to the point Nephi writes that the Nephites are destroyed. Despite the anguish of his soul, Nephi is unable to stop this. Then Nephi and the fallen Nephites watch for generations as the blessings that should have been reserved for their children are taken by the Gentiles. Is this not a hell for those involved? It appears that God uses the Gentiles to smite the Lamanites and the remaining Nephites just as Laban was struck down. On this, Nephi writes:

> After my seed and the seed of my brethren shall have dwindled in unbelief, and shall have been smitten by the Gentiles; yea, after the Lord God shall have camped against them round about, and shall have laid siege against them with a mount, and raised forts against them; and after they shall have been brought down low in the dust, even that they are not, yet the words of the righteous shall be written, and the prayers of the faithful shall be heard, and all those who have dwindled in unbelief shall not be forgotten.

Now, according to Nephi the Gentiles are white, and are initially supported by God. They should be fine, right? Nephi wrote, "And I, Nephi, beheld that the Gentiles that had gone out of captivity were delivered by the power of God out of the hands of all other nations." Indeed, we read that the Gentiles are established in the Americas by the power of the Father. But then Nephi writes:

> And the Gentiles are lifted up in **the pride** of their eyes, and have stumbled...they have built up many churches; nevertheless, they put down the power and miracles of God, and preach up unto themselves their own wisdom and their own learning, that they may get gain and **grind** upon the face of the poor. And there are many churches built up which cause envyings, and strifes, and malice. And there are also secret combinations, even as in times of old, according to the combinations of the devil, for he is the founder of all these things; yea, the founder of murder, and works of darkness; yea, and he leadeth **[the Gentiles]** by the neck with a flaxen cord, until he bindeth them with his strong cords forever.

It is then in that context, right after Nephi talks about the destruction of the Gentiles, that Nephi says God's plan is inclusive.

> For behold, my beloved brethren, I say unto you that the Lord God worketh not in darkness. He doeth not anything save it be for the benefit of the world; for he loveth the world, even that he layeth down his own life that he may draw all men unto him. Wherefore, he commandeth none that they shall not partake of his salvation.

> Behold, doth he cry unto any, saying: Depart from me? Behold, I say unto you, Nay; but he saith: Come unto me all ye ends of the earth, buy milk and honey, without money and without price... Behold, hath the Lord commanded any that they should not partake of his goodness? Behold I say unto you, Nay; but all men are privileged the one like unto the other, and none are forbidden... for he doeth that which is good among the children of men; and he doeth nothing save it be plain unto the children of men; and he inviteth them all to come unto him and partake of his goodness; and he denieth none that come unto him, black and white, bond and free, male and female; and he remembereth the heathen; and all are alike unto God, both Jew and Gentile.

If Nephi can't take these three white entities and show their rise and then destruction without teaching a lesson in humility, it is because he is preaching to deaf ears. Nephi teaches from the beginning that pride is an existential threat, and his views on race are informed by that belief.

It is no wonder that Moroni warns the Gentiles, "Therefore, repent ye, and humble yourselves before him, lest he shall come out in justice against you -- lest a remnant of the seed of Jacob shall go forth among you as a lion, and tear you in pieces, and there is none to deliver."

I do not think that Laban, the Nephites, or the Gentiles have an answer for Isaiah's question: "What mean ye? Ye beat my people to pieces, and **grind** the faces of the poor."

To sum up Nephi's view on race, Nephi is willing in wartime to stigmatize an opposing population. Nephi seemed to want separation to be able to protect and preserve his culture and thereby pass it down to his children. Regarding racial relations today, Nephi has seen events today and might not use the term **systemic racism.** He would more likely use the term **systemic genocide**. After all, he talks of the Gentiles causing the Lamanites to be "brought down low in the dust, even that they are not…."

This is a very somber topic, and unfortunately, pride and racism are topics we still deal with today.

Nephi on the Hope for the Lamanites and Their Jewish Ancestry

After all this destruction, it can be hard to remember that there is the promise of redemption. But Nephi constantly reminds us—I dare say he convinces us—that "the Lord will surely prepare a way for his people (1 Nephi 20:22)."

From there, Nephi goes on to say the Lamanites, who are people of color, will read his words and rejoice. He states that the coming of the Book of Mormon represents the start of the gathering of Israel. This will begin to resolve their subjugated status.

Oddly, Nephi writes that his descendants will rejoice at this time and will know that they came out of Jerusalem and that they are descendants of the Jews.

To me, this is very peculiar. Nephi states they are of the tribe of Joseph and not that of Judah. Scholarly apologists race to point out that the use of the term "Jews" to indicate the children of Joseph here is consistent with the term's ancient use. But even if that is true—and I have no reason to doubt that it is—the use of the term "Jew" here is not consistent with Nephi's use of the term elsewhere. Nephi has mentioned the Jews 72 times and Judah 19 times. I cannot find another time that Nephi uses "Jew" to refer to his people. And yet, now, towards the end of Nephi's writing, after he has discussed terrible calamities that fall on Israel and the subsequent redemption of Zion and the New Jerusalem, his people are on the cusp of getting their stature, strength, and knowledge back. And Nephi describes his children as Jewish. It is in that moment he says his children will rejoice and **quote** "know they are **Jews."** If we look deeper, here I think Nephi's language betrays him. I mean to say he gives away more than he intends.

We define words by experiences that are most precious to us. The things we value shape the meaning of our words, and how we use and choose them. Why would Nephi stress his people's Jewish heritage at the time of the redemption of Zion? Well, on multiple occasions, Nephi writes in detail about the redemption of Zion. On two occasions, he is forbidden from writing more. Did Nephi see something he wanted to write?

Assessing Nephi's writings on the subject alongside the Bible, we can see the issue more clearly. Permit me a healthy excerpt from Ezekiel. Like Nephi, Ezekiel mourns the fall of Jerusalem. He never stops talking about the remnant of Israel that will return. Ezekiel writes:

The hand of the Lord was upon me, and carried me ...and set me down in the midst of the valley which was full of bones...and, behold, there were very many...and...they were very dry.

And [the Lord] said unto me, Son of man, can these bones live? And I answered, O Lord God, thou knowest.

Again he said unto me, Prophesy upon these bones, and say unto them, O ye dry bones, hear the word of the Lord.

Thus saith the Lord God unto these bones; Behold, I will cause breath to enter into you, and ye shall live:

And I will lay sinews upon you, and will bring up flesh upon you, and cover you with skin, and put breath in you, and ye shall live; and ye shall know that I am the Lord.

So I prophesied as I was commanded: and as I prophesied, there was a noise, and behold a shaking, and the bones came together, bone to his bone.

And when I beheld, lo, the sinews and the flesh came up upon them, and the skin covered them above: but there was no breath in them.

Then ...saith the Lord God; Come from the four winds, O breath, and breathe upon these slain, that they may live.

So I prophesied as he commanded me, and the breath came into them, and they lived.

Then [the Lord] said unto me, Son of man, these bones are the whole house of Israel: behold, they say, Our bones are dried, and our hope is lost: we are cut off....

Thus saith the Lord God; Behold, O my people, I will open your graves, and cause you to come up out of your graves, and bring you into the land of Israel.

And ye shall know that I am the Lord, when I have opened your graves...And shall put my spirit in you, and ye shall live, and I shall place you in your own land: then shall ye know that I the Lord have spoken it, and performed it, saith the Lord.

In the context of God's word raising and gathering Israel then Ezekiel continues to mention the histories or writings of the house of Israel. Nephi understands these old writings form some of the preaching that rose Israel from the grave. Ezekiel continues:

> Moreover, thou son of man, take thee one stick, and write upon it, For Judah, and for the children of Israel his companions: then take another stick, and write upon it, For Joseph, the stick of Ephraim and for all the house of Israel his companions:

> And join them one to another into one stick; and they shall become one in thine hand.

> Thus saith the Lord God; Behold, I will take the stick of Joseph, which is in the hand of Ephraim, and the tribes of Israel his fellows, and will put them with him, even with the stick of Judah, and make them one stick, and they shall be one in mine hand.

> Thus saith the Lord God; Behold, I will take the children of Israel from among the heathen, whither they be gone, and will gather them on every side, and bring them into their own land: And I will make them one nation in the land upon the mountains of Israel; **and one king shall be king to them all**: and they shall be no more two nations, **neither shall they be divided into two kingdoms any more at all… so shall they be my people, and I will be their God.**

> **And David my servant shall be king over them;** and they all shall have one shepherd: they shall also walk in my judgments, and observe my statutes, and do them….**and my servant David shall be their prince forever.**

Ezekiel describes the redemption from hell and death that Nephi longs his people to have. Though both the Jews and Josephites will have unique roles to play, when the final goal is reached they will be one nation. This chapter in Ezekiel perfectly summarizes Nephi's words and adds dimension to them.

How can Nephi rejoice while knowing that his children suffer? What Nephi wants more than anything is for his children to be redeemed and be part of that millennial kingdom. And so we have Nephi, a descendant of Joseph with ancestry in Northern Israel, likely of Elohist persuasion, coming full circle. In his dreams, he longs to belong to that future kingdom of David. For this reason, Nephi writes that his children will rejoice when they know they are Jews in that day.

Indeed, Nephi looks forward to the time when God will "set up an ensign for the nations, and shall assemble the outcasts of Israel…." When the "envy of Ephraim departs and the adversaries of Judah shall be cut off."

This is consistent with Nephi's earlier comments. "For behold, I have workings in the spirit which doth weary me even that all my joints are weak, for those who are at Jerusalem; for had not the Lord been merciful, to show unto me concerning them, even as he had prophets of old, I should have perished also." The Jerusalem he saw must have been so wonderful that it made all his trials bearable.

Jacob says, "we knew of Christ and his kingdom, which should come." So it does seem that Nephi is referring to a future Jerusalem.

It must be a truly unimaginably wonderful kingdom indeed. Nephi waits for his own and his brother's children to be counted there. Nephi writes of his children,

"Behold, thus saith the Lord God... I covenanted with their fathers that they shall be restored (2 Nephi 10:7)."

Knowing this, it is no wonder a Latter-day Saint musician penned, "dark skin ain't a curse, it's a blessing."

Nephi's books present themselves as a proof that God lives and that there is a great history between He and Israel. Nephi also proves that Israel is not cast off or subjugated forever. "For the Lord will surely prepare a way for his people."

I hope that this study has helped you to see how very deep and plain the books of Nephi are. While I hope I have taught a lot and saved you dozens of hours of independent study, I must write that strength comes from daily prayer and pondering and study. I would encourage you to read daily so that this inspiration can yield results and then turn into whatever you want it to.

Chapter 5

Excerpts From the Triad of Witnesses

Topic	Jacob	Isaiah	Nephi
Jerusalem Destroyed	2 Nephi 6:8	2 Nephi 13:1;8	2 Nephi 25:10
Due to Wickedness Israel Will be Captive	2 Nephi 6:11	2 Nephi 15:11	2 Nephi 26:19
Details of the Savior's life	2 Nephi 10:3	2 Nephi 17: 14	2 Nephi 25:13
Israel Will Be Gathered	2 Nephi 6:11	2 Nephi 20:20	2 Nephi 29:14
Gentiles Assist with the Gathering of Israel	2 Nephi 10:8	2 Nephi 15:26; 21:12	2 Nephi 30:3
Israel's Fate Without a Redeemer	2 Nephi 9:7-9	2 Nephi 20:4	2 Nephi 28:20
Gentile Oppression is Used as a Tool in God's Hands	2 Nephi 10:18	2 Nephi 20:12	2 Nephi 26:15
Repentance is Essential	2 Nephi 9:23	2 Nephi 20:1-3	2 Nephi 31:10
Lest Israel Think Itself Cast Off Forever, the Lord Assures They Are Not	2 Nephi 10:22	2 Nephi 20:21	2 Nephi 26:15
As Israel is Gathered, the Righteous Gentiles Will be Counted Among the House of Israel	2 Nephi 10:18	2 Nephi 24:1	2 Nephi 30:2
The Fate of Those Who Fight Against Zion	2 Nephi 6:13; 10:16	2 Nephi 20:17	2 Nephi 29:14

I will end this work with quotes from the section Nephi directed at his people. Nephi wrote, "I have written what I have written and I esteem it as of great worth" I will limit my citations to what I think is within the circular that Nephi distributed which I believe is recorded in 2 Nephi 6-32. This includes words by Nephi, Isaiah, and Jacob.

As you know Nephi's definition of hell involves weakness and blindness. Israel becomes so scattered and weak that it is blind to the point it is not aware if God will help it. Israel is not aware if God still wants a relationship with it. That is to say at times Israel is not even aware if it is still a covenantal people. Nephi assures us Israel is not "cast off forever." And a careful reading shows us the mystery, "how is it possible that after having rejected the sure foundation [one] can ever build upon it…"

A more complete discussion of these specific chapters is found in the book, "The Vision of All" by Joseph Spencer. That book is written in a conversational tone and is invaluable to understand what Nephi is saying.

Here, I will only share a quote from each author on topics that all touched on. This is not an exhaustive list. This will at least provide an overview of some of the topics Nephi was so adamant about proving to his people.

All Three Write that Jerusalem is Destroyed

Nephi:

> Wherefore, it hath been told them concerning the destruction which should come upon them, immediately after my father left Jerusalem; nevertheless, they hardened their hearts; and according to my prophecy, they have been destroyed, save it be those which are carried away captive into Babylon (2 Nephi 25:10).

Isaiah:

> For behold, the Lord, the Lord of Hosts, doth take away from Jerusalem, and from Judah, the stay and the staff, the whole staff of bread, and the whole stay of water—
> For Jerusalem is ruined, and Judah is fallen, because their tongues and their doings have been against the Lord, to provoke the eyes of his glory (2 Nephi 13:1;8).

Jacob:

> And now I, Jacob, would speak somewhat concerning these words. For behold, the Lord has shown me that those who were at Jerusalem, from whence we came, have been slain and carried away captive (2 Nephi 6:8).

Due to Wickedness Israel Will be Destroyed and Made Captive

Nephi:

> And it shall come to pass, that those who have dwindled in unbelief shall be smitten by the hand of the Gentiles (2 Nephi 26:19).

Isaiah:

> Therefore, my people are gone into captivity, because they have no knowledge (2 Nephi 15:11).

Jacob:

> Wherefore, after they are driven to and fro, for thus saith the angel, many shall be afflicted in the flesh, and shall not be suffered to perish, because of the prayers of the faithful; they shall be scattered, and smitten, and hated; nevertheless, the Lord will be merciful unto them, that when they shall come to the knowledge of their Redeemer, they shall be gathered together again to the lands of their inheritance (2 Nephi 6:11).

All Three Saw the Savior and Wrote Details of the Savior's life.

Nephi:

> Behold, they will crucify him; and after he is laid in a sepulchre for the space of three days he shall rise from the dead, with healing in his wings; and all those who shall believe on his name shall be saved in the kingdom of God (2 Nephi 25:13).

Isaiah:

> Therefore, the Lord himself shall give you a sign – Behold, a virgin shall conceive, and shall bear a son, and shall call his name Immanuel (2 Nephi 17: 14).

Jacob:

> Wherefore, as I said unto you, it must needs be expedient that Christ – for in the last night the angel

spake unto me that this should be his name – should come among the Jews, ...and they shall crucify him – for thus it behooveth our God, and there is none other nation on earth that would crucify their God (2 Nephi 10:3).

Others: I mention that Nephi cites another set of three prophets in regard to details on the Savior's life. He includes this from the plates of Brass.

"And the God of our fathers, who were led out of Egypt, out of bondage, and also were preserved in the wilderness by him, yea, the God of Abraham, and of Isaac, and the God of Jacob, yieldeth himself, according to the words of the angel, as a man, into the hands of wicked men, to be lifted up, according to the words of Zenock, and to be crucified, according to the words of Neum, and to be buried in a sepulchre, according to the words of Zenos, which he spake concerning the three days of darkness, which should be a sign given of his death unto those who should inhabit the isles of the sea, more especially given unto those who are of the house of Israel (1 Nephi 19:10)."

Israel Will Be Gathered

All three authors touch on this. It seems that Israel is so lost, so scattered, and so subdued that much is written to reassure Israel that the ancient covenants still apply. I do not do justice to these passages as they are not appreciated without their full context.

Nephi:

And it shall come to pass that my people, which are of the house of Israel, shall be gathered home unto the lands of their possessions; and my word also shall be gathered in one (2 Nephi 29:14).

Isaiah:

And it shall come to pass in that day, that the remnant of Israel, and such as are escaped of the house of Jacob, shall no more again stay upon him that smote them, but shall stay upon the Lord, the Holy One of Israel, in truth (2 Nephi 20:20).

Jacob:

And behold, according to the words of the prophet, the Messiah will set himself again the second time to recover them; wherefore, he will manifest himself unto them in power and great glory, unto the destruction of their enemies, when that day cometh when they shall believe in him; and none will he destroy that believe in him (2 Nephi 6:11).

Gentiles Assist with the Gathering of Israel

Nephi:

And now, I would prophesy somewhat more concerning the Jews and the Gentiles. For after the book of which I have spoken shall come forth, and be written unto the Gentiles, and sealed up again unto the Lord, there shall be many which shall believe the words which are written; and they shall carry them forth unto the remnant of our seed (2 Nephi 30:3).

Isaiah:

And he will lift up an ensign to the nations from far, and will hiss unto them from the end of the earth; and behold, they shall come with speed swiftly; none shall be weary nor stumble among them. And he shall set up an ensign for the nations, and shall assemble the outcasts of Israel, and gather together the dispersed of Judah from the four corners of the earth. (2 Nephi 15:26, 21:12).

There are phrases more supportive of this concept in Isaiah such as those found in Isaiah 60. It may seem surprising that Nephi doesn't cite Isaiah 60. However, scholars point out Nephi did not likely have access to the last part of Isaiah as it was compiled after 600 BCE.

Jacob:

> And it shall come to pass that they shall be gathered in from their long dispersion, from the isles of the sea, and from the four parts of the earth; and the nations of the Gentiles shall be great in the eyes of me, saith God, in carrying them forth to the lands of their inheritance (2 Nephi 10:8).

Our Fate Without a Redeemer

Nephi:

> For behold, at that day shall [the devil] rage in the hearts of the children of men, and stir them up to anger against that which is good (2 Nephi 28:20).

Isaiah:

> Without me they shall bow down under the prisoners, and they shall fall under the slain (2 Nephi 20:4).

Jacob:

> O the wisdom of God, his mercy and grace! For behold, if the flesh should rise no more our spirits must become subject to that angel who fell from before the presence of the Eternal God, and became the devil, to rise no more. And our spirits must have become like unto him, and we become devils, angels to a devil, to be shut out from the presence of our God, and to remain with the father of lies, in misery, like unto himself; yea...who...stirreth up the children of men unto secret combinations of murder and all manner of secret works of darkness (2 Nephi 9:7-9).

Gentile Oppression is Used as a Tool in God's Hands

Nephi:

>   After my seed and the seed of my brethren shall have dwindled in unbelief, and shall have been smitten by the Gentiles; yea, after the Lord God shall have camped against them round about, and shall have laid siege against them with a mount, and raised forts against them; and after they shall have been brought down low in the dust, even that they are not, yet the words of the righteous shall be written, and the prayers of the faithful shall be heard, and all those who have dwindled in unbelief shall not be forgotten (2 Nephi 26:15).

Isaiah:

>   Wherefore it shall come to pass that when the Lord hath performed his whole work upon Mount Zion and upon Jerusalem, I will punish the fruit of the stout heart of the king of Assyria, and the glory of his high looks (2 Nephi 20:12).

Jacob:

>   Wherefore, my beloved brethren, thus saith our God: I will afflict thy seed by the hand of the Gentiles; nevertheless, I will soften the hearts of the Gentiles, that they shall be like unto a father to them; wherefore, the Gentiles shall be blessed and numbered among the house of Israel (2 Nephi 10:18).

Repentance is Essential

Nephi:

>   And he said unto the children of men: Follow thou me. Wherefore, my beloved brethren, can we follow Jesus save we shall be willing to keep the commandments of the Father? (2 Nephi 31:10).

Isaiah:

> Wo unto them that decree unrighteous decrees, and
> that write grievousness which they have prescribed; To
> turn away the needy from judgment, and to take away
> the right from the poor of my people, that widows may
> be their prey, and that they may rob the fatherless! (2
> Nephi 20:1-3).

Jacob:

> And he commandeth all men that they must repent,
> and be baptized in his name, having perfect faith in the
> Holy One of Israel, or they cannot be saved in the
> kingdom of God (2 Nephi 9:23).

Lest Israel Think Itself Cast Off Forever, the Lord Assures They Are Not

Nephi:

> The prayers of the faithful shall be heard, and all those
> who have dwindled in unbelief shall not be forgotten (2
> Nephi 26:15).

Isaiah:

> The remnant shall return, yea, even the remnant of
> Jacob, unto the mighty God (2 Nephi 20:21).

Jacob:

> For behold, the Lord God has led away from time to
> time from the house of Israel, according to his will and
> pleasure. And now behold, the Lord remembereth all
> them who have been broken off, wherefore he
> remembereth us also (2 Nephi 10:22).

As Israel is Gathered, the Righteous Gentiles Will be Counted Among the House of Israel

Nephi:

> For behold, I say unto you that as many of the Gentiles
> as will repent are the covenant people of the Lord; and
> as many of the Jews as will not repent shall be cast off;

for the Lord covenanteth with none save it be with them that repent and believe in his Son, who is the Holy One of Israel (2 Nephi 30:2).

Isaiah:

For the Lord will have mercy on Jacob, and will yet choose Israel, and set them in their own land; and the strangers shall be joined with them, and they shall cleave to the house of Jacob (2 Nephi 24:1).

Jacob:

I will soften the hearts of the Gentiles, that they shall be like unto a father to them; wherefore, the Gentiles shall be blessed and numbered among the house of Israel (2 Nephi 10:18).

The Fate of Those Who Fight Against Zion

Nephi:

I will show unto them that fight against my word and against my people, who are of the house of Israel, that I am God, and that I covenanted with Abraham that I would remember his seed forever (2 Nephi 29:14).

Isaiah:

And the light of Israel shall be for a fire, and his Holy One for a flame, and shall burn and shall devour his thorns and his briers in one day (2 Nephi 20:17).

Jacob:

Wherefore, they that fight against Zion and the covenant people of the Lord shall lick up the dust of their feet; and the people of the Lord shall not be ashamed. For the people of the Lord are they who wait for him; for they still wait for the coming of the Messiah (2 Nephi 6:13).

And he that fighteth against Zion shall perish, saith God (2 Nephi 10:13).

Conclusion

To conclude I would like to write what this all meant to the people who heard it. While I have expressed the perspectives Nephi offers, I have tried to detail a few of the implications of such perspectives. We have talked about what good is, what evil is, what God's plans are, and many other things.

Ultimately the righteous of Nephi's descendants had a living relationship with God. That is to say, they did not just try to be good so that they would get to heaven when they die. Yes. They did expect to go to heaven when they die. But, far from having a distant God who might check in after death, their relationship with God was very alive with real-time benefits, sorrows, gifts, and blessings.

Mormon characterized the Christian faith of Nephi's children during a desperate time in their history:

> **And this was their faith**... if they were faithful in keeping the commandments of God that he would prosper them in the land; yea, warn them to flee, or to prepare for war, according to their danger; And also, that God would make it known unto them whither they should go to defend themselves against their enemies, and by so doing, the Lord would deliver them."

This was the faith Nephi shared. He believed in a God that wants to have an active and living relationship with all. Nephi shows us the way he developed that relationship and the value it was to him. His imperfections give us proof that we too are acceptable, loved, and even cherished by God. Ultimately Nephi teaches us we can trust God despite our imperfections, and he shows how to access this relationship. Just like any relationship, we must check in regularly. It is a very easy and small thing to just try and to read scriptures daily. A later Nephite prophet wrote that it is as easy to give heed to the word of Christ as it was for Nephi to look at his compass. Just as Ezekiel saw, the bones of Israel heard the Word, and their flesh and breath were restored. Likewise, this is my faith: if we just nourish our spirit **every day,** if we just realign our direction once a day we will, like Nephi, progress as we are led to a sure future. We will become strong, prosper in all our goals, and we will grow in wisdom and agency. While I may have saved you dozens of hours reading, I haven't done any favors. It is the Book of Mormon and the Bible that are designed to give strength, make one rejoice, and have faith. While it is likely impossible for you to know that now, after months or years of daily reading and continued growth, who can look back and dispute?

Appendix 1

That They May Rejoice-

Rhetorical Tools Nephi May Have Used.
Unlocking the inspiration hidden in Nephite literary techniques

Summary:

While Mormon saw the fall of his nation and people he saw records that were "choice" to him.[171] One might ask what could possibly appear inspiring, wonderful or, "choice" to a person so affected by trauma and personal loss. What could inspire Mormon in the face of so much destruction? When we read the small plates of Nephi (to which Mormon referred) do we get similar inspiration? I propose we often do not. And yet, the inspiration we do not see is hidden in plain sight.

As one culture attempts to understand another, logistical issues arise in translation and subsequently when interpreting the translated text. The functional equivalence of one phrase may be completely lost if not a priority in translating. Based on comparative analysis I propose the Nephites differentiated between high fidelity and paraphrastic citations. The aim of this appendix is to attempt to identify the locution used to designate the level of fidelity in a citation. I hold that the only parts of Nephi's writing that should be considered a citation of

---

[171] Words of Mormon 1:6

Isaiah in the modern sense is 2 Nephi 12-24. This is likely all very intentional by Nephi. It follows that the second book of Nephi is best understood as a witness document. Additionally, the importance of identifying paraphrased text is highlighted with the example of 1 Nephi 21. This demonstrates additional literary techniques such as: weaving terms and allusions in with the current text, changing the frame of reference from which the scripture is understood, giving additional prophecies based on new situations, juxtaposing the current situation with the past and future, juxtaposing opposing emotions and experiences, and the use of repetition and metric devices. These were the tools the nascent Nephite nation used to confront reality. They can continue to inspire today.

Background

Largely, Western culture often declares it taboo to change or modify art, including literature and poetry. Touching on this, anthropologist Dennis Tedlock, for example, contrasted Western and Mayan civilizations, "to paraphrase the lines of a finished poem would be what modern Western critics have called a 'heresy,' but paraphrase is the method by which Mayans construct poems in the first place."[172] Certainly sacred writing may be viewed by laypersons as "finished" and therefore unalterable.

Other cultures (such as the Mayans) provide an example of a more fluid approach to internalizing art, including written texts. Another example is found within certain eastern cultures. Chaplain Brian Steed of the U.S. Army

---

[172] Dennis Tedlock, *2000 Years of Mayan literature* (Berkeley, CA: University of California Press, 2010), 2

describes meetings in Jordan in which he noted that all present spoke the same words, formed the same sentences, and made the same points but with variations. He wrote, "an American would typically see this as a wasted forty minutes or so, but the Arabs understood they all had a right to make those remarks regardless of who else had said them." [173] Such a pseudo-recitation is meaningful as it shows personal internalization of the topic at hand. Additionally, when the group allows each person time to speak - even in a manner that we would consider nearly redundant - it offers inclusion.

Another setting in which modification of text is considered positive, even crucial is the process of likening. In Nephite literature the concept is never defined. This absence implies Nephi's audience is familiar with their own process of likening. Perhaps to liken is to modify text to make it more understandable, however as I cannot be sure, in the present I will refer to *any* text that is modified in *any* way as paraphrased.

Nephi, the founder of the Nephite nation, was a writer for all time, but also a writer *of* his time. Therefore, some of the concepts and methods he employs were so well-known by his immediate audience as to make their explicit definition unnecessary or even condescending. Since the Book of Mormon is the story of a fallen people,[174] in retrospection we are left to wonder what represented common knowledge among the members of the fallen nation.

---

[173] Brian L. Steed, *Bees and spiders: Applied Cultural Awareness and the art of cross-cultural influence* (Houston, TX: Strategic Book Publishing and Rights Co., 2014), 63.
[174] D&C 20:9

Today it is universally recognized that quotation marks can indicate a verbatim quotation. On the other hand, a paraphrase is not designated with quotation marks. Within Nephite society there was also a manner to designate between a verbatim citation and a paraphrase. However, today we are blind to these designations.[175,176]

Yet if we compare similar passages and look at the text surrounding them, it will become clear what designates a citation. Isaiah is often cited in the Book of Mormon, therefore great insights can be obtained about Nephite literary techniques by comparing repetitive occurrences of Isaiah verses. We don't have the original text or source material but, presumably, if there is a text reproduced *identically* to another text it is possible the translator's intent was to imply a citation.[177] Here then is the key: intentional modifications in the text can be understood to occur when changes are present in only *one* copy of a verse that has multiple citations.

---

[175] Skousen proposed that whenever 16 or more consecutive identical words were shared between The Book of Mormon and the Bible, this should constitute a citation. Royal Skousen, The History of the Text of The Book of Mormon Part 5, The King James Quotations in The Book of Mormon (KJQ) 2019 pg 16

[176] Other approaches have been taken to include consensus from manual comparison by multiple investigators. John A. Tvedtnes, *The Isaiah Variants in The Book of Mormon* (Provo, UT: Foundation for Ancient Research and Mormon Studies, 1981).

[177] Certainly the English terms have no direct correlation with the original text. However, one presumes there is an association in some manner.

KJV (original)	High-Fidelity Citation	Paraphrastic Citation
Isaiah 11:4	**2 Nephi 21:4**	**2 Nephi 30:9**
But with righteousness shall he judge the poor, and reprove with equity for the meek of the earth: and he shall smite the earth with the rod of his mouth, and with the breath of his lips shall he slay the wicked.	But with righteousness shall he judge the poor, and reprove with equity for the meek of the earth; and he shall smite the earth with the rod of his mouth, and with the breath of his lips shall he slay the wicked.	*And* with righteousness shall *the Lord God* judge the poor, and reprove with equity for the meek of the earth. And he shall smite the earth with the rod of his mouth; and with the breath of his lips shall he slay the wicked.
Isaiah 11:6	**2 Nephi 21:6**	**2 Nephi 30:12**
The wolf also shall dwell with the lamb, and the leopard shall lie down with the kid; and the calf and the young lion and the fatling together; and a little child shall lead them.	The wolf also shall dwell with the lamb, and the leopard shall lie down with the kid, and the calf and the young lion and the fatling together; and a little child shall lead them.	*And then* shall the wolf dwell with the lamb; and the leopard shall lie down with the kid, and the calf, and the young lion, and the fatling, together; and a little child shall lead them.
Isaiah 49:25	**1 Nephi 21:25**	**2 Nephi 6:17**
But thus saith the Lord, Even the captives of the mighty shall be taken away, and the prey of the terrible shall be delivered: for I will contend with him that contendeth with thee, and I will save thy children.	But thus saith the Lord, even the captives of the mighty shall be taken away, and the prey of the terrible shall be delivered; for I will contend with him that contendeth with thee, and I will save thy children.	But thus saith the Lord: Even the captives of the mighty shall be taken away, and the prey of the terrible shall be delivered; for *the Mighty God shall deliver his covenant people. For thus saith the Lord:* I will contend with them that contendeth with me
Isaiah 52:7	**Mosiah 12:21**	**1 Nephi 13:37**
How beautiful upon the mountains are the feet of him that bringeth good tidings, that publisheth peace; that bringeth good tidings of good, that publisheth salvation; that saith unto Zion, Thy God reigneth!	How beautiful upon the mountains are the feet of him that bringeth good tidings; that publisheth peace; that bringeth good tidings of good; that publisheth salvation; that saith unto Zion, Thy God reigneth;	*and whoso shall* publish peace, *yea*, tidings *of great joy*, how beautiful upon the mountains *shall they be.*
Isaiah 52:8	**Mosiah 12:22**	**Mosiah 15:29**
Thy watchmen shall lift up the voice; with the voice together shall they sing: for they shall see eye to eye, when the Lord shall bring again Zion.	Thy watchmen shall lift up the voice; with the voice together shall they sing; for they shall see eye to eye when the Lord shall bring again Zion;	*Yea, Lord*, thy watchmen shall lift up their voice; with the voice together shall they sing; for they shall see eye to eye, when the Lord shall bring again Zion.

Table 3: Verses in which Isaiah text is apparently reproduced on multiple occasions. High-fidelity citations are identical in every case to the KJV Isaiah base text (keep in mind a cultural and creative translation process). Paraphrastic citations have changed text demonstrated in *italics*.

Table 3 depicts verses that are cited twice and compares them to the KJV (the base text of the Book of Mormon). There are occasions when Isaiah's words are cited in a different manner than the original (third column). These paraphrastic citations demonstrate that the Nephites at times modify the text. While all of these examples are instructive on many levels, for now I want to only establish the idea that both high-fidelity and paraphrastic citations exist. That is to say, at times a Nephite orator may reference another's words without giving a verbatim quote.

Presentation of High-Fidelity Citations

Let us turn to the wording surrounding these scriptures. The citations identified as high-fidelity in table 3 are introduced with the following:

> **now** *these are the words* [178]

> but thus saith the Lord[179]

> **what meaneth** *the words which* **are written**, and which have been taught by our fathers, saying[180]

In two of these cases we see a determiner. The definite article is used: "these are **the words**" or, "**the words which** are written." In both cases of high-fidelity citation the term "words" is used as a direct object.[181]

---

[178] 2 Nephi 11:8 prior to Isaiah 2-14 citation (2 Nephi 12-24). Emphasis added.

[179] 1 Nephi 21:25 at the beginning of Isaiah 49:25 citation.

[180] Mosiah 12:20 prior to the high-fidelity citation of Isaiah 52:7-10. Emphasis added.

[181] This is not to say there is Hebrew or Egyptian equivalent in syntax and grammar. Rather, I submit that just as a start codon such as "AUG" precedes an area of transcription, likewise, the translator portrays the citation locution using the described convention.

Notice that words are referenced as an object, as if they are their own entity or record. This may make sense of other Nephite societal constructs. For example, on one occasion Mormon writes, "and now the words of Amulek are not all written, nevertheless a part of his words are written in this book." [182] Nephi likewise writes, "And now, Jacob spake many more things to my people at that time…"[183] These verses may seem strange to the reader. Why is this clarification present? Did the reader truly expect an *exhaustive* account of every word spoken by Amulek when preaching to an entire city over many weeks? Or, did the reader expect every word uttered by Jacob at a multi-day conference to be written? Of course not. And yet, both Mormon and Nephi feel obliged to excuse themselves for only giving a partial record. We can infer two things. There must be a record that contains something defined as "the words of Amulek's mission in Ammonihah" and "the words of Jacob" in that specific conference. Further, Mormon and Nephi must have implied at some point in the record that they *were* giving a complete record. This then is the reason Mormon and Nephi feel obliged to state the words of Amulek and Jacob are only a partial account.

What did Mormon and Nephi write that implied that they were giving a complete record (and thereby necessitating clarification that the account was not complete)? As expected, there is verbiage consistent with high-fidelity citations. At the start of the citations we read:

> Now ***these are the words*** which Amulek preached…[184]

---

[182] Alma 9:34. Emphasis added.
[183] 2 Nephi 11:1
[184] Alma 10:1. Emphasis added.

> *The words of Jacob*, the brother of Nephi, which he
> spake unto the people of Nephi[185]

In both cases we see a determiner and a reference to words as a direct object. It follows "the words" indicate a defined record.

We need to examine paraphrastic citations to observe how they are introduced.

Presentation of Paraphrastic Isaiah Citations

We will now turn our attention to words introducing the paraphrastic citations in table 3. By assuming there is *some* degree of correlation between the English text and the source material we presume the paraphrastic citations recorded on the plates in column 3 of table 3 are different than those in column 2.

This is how the citations are introduced:

> *I* would speak unto you[186]
>
> But thus saith the Lord [187]
>
> For, behold, saith the Lamb[188]
>
> And now *Abinadi said* unto them[189]
>
> *I* say unto you[190]

In the case of Abinadi's citation, why might Mormon bother clarifying the altered Isaiah citation is spoken by Abinadi? Perhaps he did not want Abinadi's intent to be lost. Abinadi in the custom of the day personalizes the

---

[185] 2 Nephi 6:1. Emphasis added.
[186] 2 Nephi 30:1
[187] 2 Nephi 6:17
[188] 1 Nephi 13:35
[189] Mosiah 15:1
[190] Mosiah 15:11

scripture. The original reads, "Thy watchmen shall lift up their voice." Abinadi states, "*Yea, Lord,* thy watchmen shall lift up their voice..." By including, "*Yea, Lord...*" Abinadi appears to make the verse into a prayer. One must also question if part of Abinadi's martyrdom speech is in part a conversation between Abinadi and the Lord. Aside from that, in the original, "Thy watchmen" refers to Zion's watchmen. Consistent with Abinadi's message, he is also stating that the Lord is an embodiment of Zion. Such a modification is not likely made lightly, and it depicts the verse had a personal meaning to Abinadi.

The Savior also appears to follow Nephite convention when talking to them. Prior to citing clear variants of Isaiah (verses different from His own prior citation) He states, "And verily *I* say unto you..." [191]

In each of these paraphrastic citations Mormon or the speaker and sometimes both ensure to clarify this is *another* person speaking. I clarify that I am terming these citations "paraphrastic" because they appear to contain deviations from the known Isaiah text that the Nephites possessed (this is evident because of the existence of the high-fidelity citations). However, these paraphrastic Isaiah citations likely represent high-fidelity citations relative to the person speaking (e.g., Nephi, Abinadi, and Jesus Christ).

Furthermore, the term 'paraphrastic' may have a negative connotation. That should not be the case. These paraphrastic citations could equally be referred to as examples of intertextuality or likening. I use the term 'paraphrastic' to emphasize that the Nephites do indeed

---

[191] 3 Nephi 21:1

appear to differentiate between high-fidelity and paraphrastic citations of source material. It is notable that in each paraphrase a source other than Isaiah was named. I do not believe that was happenstance but was the result of careful record keeping. I hold that the textual designation of specifying another speaker as citing the original author indicates a paraphrastic citation.[192]

Examples of Embedded Citations Presented with High-Fidelity Locution

Grant Hardy wrote of the Book of Mormon that, "recurring expressions may simply be random, but it is also possible to read some of them as intentional."[193]

That high-fidelity citations are notated by referring to them as objects seems generally consistent throughout the rest of Nephite culture. Others continue to refer to writings as direct objects. They are a defined entity. Moroni would write, "**An epistle** of my father..."[194] He also wrote, "**The words** of Christ..."[195] and "**The manner** of administering the wine..."[196] Some of the presumed citations such as epistles are introduced with high-fidelity notation: "Lachoneus... received an epistle from the leader and the governor of this band of robbers; and **these were the words**..."[197] Prior to citing Captain Moroni's letter to Pahoran, Mormon writes, "**these are the words**

---

[192] This will explain many of the variants in 2 Nephi 7-8 since they are specifically identified as the words of Jacob.
[193] Grant Hardy Understanding The Book of Mormon: A Reader's Guide page 248
[194] Moroni 8:1
[195] Moroni 2:1
[196] Moroni 5:1
[197] 3 Nephi 3:1

which he wrote..." [198] Prior to Pahoran's response we read, "**And these are the words** which he received." Prior to Helaman's letter to Captain Moroni we read, "**these are the words** which he wrote..." [199] Therefore it seems with these examples the same notation was used during much of Nephite history. Moroni perhaps modifies 'words' to 'epistle.' There is always a determinant and direct object.

It would be amiss to not include the most essential citations. It goes without say that of all the words in the Book of Mormon, the words of Christ would be least likely to be modified. Accordingly every citation has high-fidelity notation we read:

> When Jesus had spoken **these words** [200] (8 occurrences)
>
> When he had said **these words** [201]
>
> **Those same words** which Jesus had spoken [202]
>
> When Jesus had said **these words** [203]
>
> when Jesus had told **these things** [204]

Finally, at the end of the Jesus' ministry to the Nephites, Mormon references the "words of Jesus" multiple times. [205] Therefore, nearly without exception after every citation, Christ's words are introduced as "the words" or "these words." The high frequency of that type of notation alone surrounding the words of Christ indicate the manner of writing is significant in Nephite custom.

---

[198] Alma 60:1
[199] Alma 56:2
[200] 3 Nephi 12:1; 14:1; 15:11; 17:1; 18:17, 26; 19:30; 28:12
[201] 3 Nephi 17:21; 18:8
[202] 3 Nephi 19:8
[203] 3 Nephi 23:6; 28:1
[204] 3 Nephi 26:1
[205] 3 Nephi 28:34

It appears that Mormon is deliberate and systematic about indicating when a high-fidelity citation is used, and he attributes the citation to the appropriate party. I hold that in the absence of notation indicating a high-fidelity, the text should not be considered a verbatim citation.

Introduction to Likening

Immediately prior to 2 Nephi 12, Nephi writes, "Now *these are the words* and ye may liken them unto you."[206] Consistent with our earlier discussion, this qualification seems to imply that the following words are the originals and have not yet been changed or "likened."[207] In contrast, prior to less formal citations of Isaiah Nephi instead mentions that he will apply the scriptures and "liken them" to his people. This may imply some sort of change or paraphrase in the oral reproduction of the text if not the written text as well. Nephi writes, "*after this manner* has the prophet written…"[208] Comparatively, this appears to be an assertion that Nephi will *not* transliterate Isaiah's words verbatim. Unsurprisingly, scholars have suggested the variants found in 1 Nephi 20 may comprise intentional changes from the source material to apply the text to the Nephites' specific situation.[209]

Our difficulty in understanding likening is that Nephi does not ever explain precisely what likening is. Scribes acted as both author and copyist in First Temple times. We do not know all of their adaptation techniques.

---

[206] 2 Ne 11:8
[207] A discussion regarding the definition of the term likening will follow.
[208] 1 Nephi 19:24; 20:1
[209] Joseph M. Spencer, *The Vision of All: Twenty-Five Lectures on Isaiah in Nephi's Record*, Contemporary Studies in Scripture (Salt Lake City: Greg Kofford Books, 2016).

Nephi's original audience was likely familiar with the concept of likening. Nephi invites his audience to liken the scriptures to themselves but does not describe the practice. If likening does involve modifying or updating text, then the present analysis perhaps gives a place to start a discussion on likening. Having identified which passages from Isaiah are transmitted with high degrees of fidelity to their source and which have been handled with more artistic freedom, we are now able to determine which texts have been potentially altered.

However, it is almost certain that Nephi employed more than one literary technique. Therefore, while we may identify paraphrastic passages, it is another work altogether to define the literary mechanisms at work and correctly attribute which mechanisms contributed to which changes. Therefore, I prefer the term "paraphrastic citation" to encompass all forms of potential changes that may occur in the process of handing down text over generations.

Potential Meanings of "Likening"

To continue our discussion on likening specifically, I will mention that Nephi, Jacob, and Jesus Christ are the only figures that use the word "liken" in the Book of Mormon. In some cases it appears that to liken means to compare. Christ states,

> Therefore, whoso heareth these sayings of mine and doeth them, I will *liken* him unto a wise man... (emphasis added).[210]

---

[210] 3 Nephi 14:24

The usage in Joseph Smith's day as well suggests that to liken is to compare. On one occasion he stated:

> I take my ring from my finger and *liken* it unto the mind of man, the immortal spirit, because it has no beginning. Suppose you cut it in two; but as the Lord lives there would be an end (emphasis added).[211]

When thinking of Nephi's time, it appears that liken also means to compare. Nephi discusses Isaiah's description of Latter-day events:

> [T]he Lord God will proceed to do a marvelous work among the Gentiles, which shall be of great worth unto our seed; wherefore, it is *likened* unto their being nourished by the Gentiles and being carried in their arms and upon their shoulders (emphasis added).[212]

In all three uses here the word "likened," appears to function to denote a comparison. As I review modern scholarly articles, I do not find a consensus definition of the term "to liken." Some have described the process of likening as "a rhetorical and poetic device in which one text alludes to an earlier text in a way that evokes resonances of the earlier text beyond those explicitly cited."[213] Nephi is certainly doing that with frequent allusions to Isaiah. Others have written Nephi's likening "is a question of taking the ... text as a kind of template for making sense of one's own experience and vision.

---

[211] *General conference of the church, Minutes, and JS, Discourses, Nauvoo, Hancock Co.*, IL, 6–7 Apr. 1844; in "Conference Minutes, Times and Seasons, 15 Aug. 1844, 5:615. site: https://www.josephsmithpapers.org/paper-summary/minutes-and-discourses-6-7-april-1844-as-published-in-times-and-seasons/13

[212] 1 Nephi 22:8

[213] Richard B. Hays, *The Conversion of the Imagination: Paul as Interpreter of Israel's Scripture* (Grand Rapids, MI: William B. Eerdmans, 2005), 2.

...involves taking a past text as a guide for faithfully recasting the present."[214]

To me it seems Nephi adds details as he likens[215] and he observes and re-applies patterns in God's dealings.[216] Complicating the issue is that different Nephite prophets liken Isaiah's words with different methods and intent.[217] Likening can occur on an individual basis or on a communal basis.[218] Joseph Spencer wrote, "likening a text is, for Nephi, a question of weaving into the scriptural text ...[the] truths one has learned regarding the meaning and importance of the Abrahamic covenant through some kind of revelatory or prophetic experience. It might thus be said that it is only a prophet—though that word must be taken in its broadest definitions referring to anyone

---

[214] Joseph M. Spencer Jenny Web *Reading Nephi Reading Isaiah: 2 Nephi 26-27* Brigham Young University BYU Scholars Archive Maxwell Institute Publications 2016
[215] Donald W. Parry, John W. Welch *Isaiah in The Book of Mormon* – Neal A. Maxwell Institute for Religious Scholarship November 1, 1997, 209
[216] Ibid., 201-202
[217] "...both Nephi and Abinadi formulate their respective approaches to typology in the course of reading Isaiah. But, because they understand the task of (Isaiah's) prophecy so distinctively, they arrive at quite different understandings of typology. For both, typology is a question of knowing how to read scripture in a uniquely Christian way, but what is to be read typologically is different for each of them. This seems, in the end, to be a consequence of Nephi's having discovered his understanding of typology in the complexly structured writings of Isaiah, while Abinadi apparently brought his understanding of typology to the writings of Isaiah. More explicitly, Nephi draws from Isaiah an understanding of the relationship between the Law of Moses and the Messiah that fits Isaiah's heavy emphasis on the Israelite covenant, while Abinadi imposes on Isaiah an understanding of the relationship between the Law and the Messiah that effectively ignores Isaiah's focus on covenantal questions" Joseph M. Spencer, "An Other Testament: On Typology" (2016). *Maxwell Institute Publications 8* https://scholarsarchive.byu.edu/mi
[218] Alan Goff Likening in The Book of Mormon A Look at Joseph M. Spencer's An Other Testament: On Typology BYU Studies Quarterly volume 52 number 4

who has "the spirit of prophecy" (see 2 Nephi 25:4)—who can authoritatively give new life to [i.e., liken] a scriptural text."[219]

Complicating the definition of the term "to liken," I will point out here that Strong's concordance states three possible words that can be translated as "to liken." These are, "damah", "shavah", and "mashal."[220,221,222] Each of these verbs occur preciously few times in the Old Testament, which makes comparative analysis almost impossible. While all three verbs may mean, "to compare," it seems reasonable that it was different cultural practices that necessitated the existence of three distinct words, each of which clearly have different roots. Therefore while we read the term "liken" in multiple verses the source material may be referring to different concepts. Additionally, Nephi's training in the First Temple period was less influenced by Hellenistic and Babylonian influences when compared with the Second Temple period. Therefore even should a consensus among scholars exist regarding the term "to liken" it is possible the definition of the term hearkens to a different era.

Regardless, consistent with the scribal culture of Nephi's day, it would likely be unnatural for Nephi if he didn't update or modify text. Presumably any change would be made to increase understanding of the listeners and could be construed as a form of "likening."

In modern usage Latter-day Saints today are taught in Preach My Gospel, "to "liken" is to create a mental bridge

---

[219] Spencer, *Reading Nephi Reading Isaiah: 2 Nephi 26-27*

[220] Strong's Hebrew: 1819. דָּמָה (damah) -- to be like, resemble (biblehub.com)

[221] Strong's Hebrew: 7737. שָׁוָה (shavah) -- avail (biblehub.com)

[222] Strong's Hebrew: 4911. מָשַׁל (mashal) -- like (biblehub.com)

between understanding the doctrine and living the doctrine."[223] This appears to encompass multiple methodologies as well. Whether likening includes comparing, alluding, appropriating, re-applying, adding to text, understanding doctrine or finally whether likening constitutes a new revelation itself requires additional investigation. And this is an essential point if we are to liken the scriptures.

It appears the term 'to liken' may include multiple ancient concepts as it has multiple roots. Further, at least one definition of 'to liken' appears to be an inclusive umbrella that encompasses any technique or subordinate process aimed at achieving understanding.

1 Nephi 21: Case Study in Paraphrastic Text

When comparing 1 Nephi 21 to Isaiah 49, there are a few *additional* phrases found in 1 Nephi 21. I believe many Latter-day Saints would opine that the extra phrases found in 1 Nephi 21 were likely in Isaiah's original work but that malicious hands removed the phrases from the original before it came down to us. Nephi has certainly commented on parts of scripture being removed by evil individuals.[224] However, given that entire scrolls are missing, probability suggests that statements regarding the removal of scripture refers to at least one of dozens of books that are alluded to in canonized works, but that have not survived for us to read.[225] That is to say,

---

[223] *Preach My Gospel.* Salt Lake City, UT: The Church of Jesus Christ of Latter-day Saints, 2004, pp 23-46

[224] 1 Nephi 13:26-40

[225] Dozens of complete books are lost. For a partial list see "Lost Books of Scripture," The Church of Jesus Christ of Latter-day Saints, accessed September 11, 2022,
https://abn.churchofjesuschrist.org/study/scriptures/gs/scriptures?lang=eng

unfortunately, far more than the few lines of text we will discuss here were potentially lost. Regardless, the additional lines in 1 Nephi 21 could represent Isaiah's brilliance that nefarious individuals censored or, alternatively, the lines represent the work of Nephi's molding and likening of the text. In any case, it may be instructive to consider what these extra words are and ask what they contribute. But, Nephi himself says that he did liken these words[226].

It is reasonable that to liken implies some sort of modification. Again, he also omits high-fidelity citations markers that would be readily identifiable to his audience. It is reasonable then to interpret the differences in 1 Nephi 21 as Nephi's *own* additions. I have listed added lines in table 4.

Phrases in 1 Nephi 21 Not Found in Isaiah 49

And again: Hearken, O ye house of Israel, all ye that are broken off and are driven out because of the wickedness of the pastors of my people; yea, all ye that are broken off, that are scattered abroad, who are of my people. O house of Israel. (vs 1)
O isles of the sea, (vs 8)
O house of Israel, behold, these shall come from far; and lo, these from the north and the west; and these from the land of Sinim. (vs 12)
Sing, O heavens; and be joyful, O earth; *for the feet of those who are in the east shall be established;* and break forth into singing, O mountains; *for they shall be smitten no more;* For the Lord hath comforted his people, and will have mercy upon his afflicted. But, behold, Zion hath said: The Lord hath forsaken me, and my Lord hath forgotten me- *but he will show you that he hath not.* For can a woman forget her sucking child, that she should not have compassion on the son of her womb? Yea, they may forget, yet will I not forget thee, *O house of Israel.* (vs 13-16)

---

[226] 1 Nephi 19:23

Let us for a moment appreciate the words that Nephi added. We are finally getting a clear albeit partial display of Nephi's rhetorical skills. Recall that his writing does not carry the weight of his oratory skills.[227]

Consider the band of refugees which forms Nephi's people at this point. They have left Jerusalem. They have crossed the ocean and the reality of their situation is becoming more gravely clear. Some of them feel they will forever wander as a lonesome and a solemn people.[228] Nephi likens their plight to a well-known story so "that [his hearers] may have hope."[229] Nephi reads or says,

> *Hearken, O ye **house** of Israel, all ye that are **broken off** and are **driven out** because of the wickedness of the pastors of my people; yea, all ye that are **broken off**, that are **scattered** abroad, who are of my people **O house** of Israel…*

Nephi does not pretend that things are going well. He addresses the issue head-on. "House of Israel" in this setting appears to reference his people's history. In that setting, a group of exiles would certainly not intuitively feel like the Kingdom of Israel or House of Israel. "House of Israel" alludes in this case to the strength and togetherness of Israel. When they were together, they were a mighty kingdom, the envy of the world.[230] Not only was Israel delivered from the slavery of Egypt but it had established a united monarchy. The prosperity of Israel was such that it could perform large-scale and long-

---

[227] 2 Nephi 33:1
[228] Jacob 7:26.
[229] 1 Nephi 19:24
[230] Such was the prosperity of Israel that persons such as the Queen of Sheba were initially incredulous (1 Kings 10:7).

term operations hundreds of kilometers from Jerusalem on the very borders of neighboring powers. This is evidenced by thousands of now abandoned mining sites.[231]

I imagine that as Nephi referred to his people as "house of Israel," it may have been perceived as ironic or even sardonic. They are scattered Israel, not a house. It is possible his people no longer viewed themselves as the house of Israel.[232] Nephi has just juxtaposed their doubt with an emphasis four times over that they are broken off from their home (*broken* off, *driven* out, *scattered*, *broken* off). They are scattered and driven away. This is not getting any happier.

But, lest their minds fall into overwhelming self-doubt or perhaps guilt, Nephi reminds them the situation is not their fault. This is because of the *pastors* of the people, an allusion that also certainly brings up multiple memories. Nephi then says again for a second time in verse 1, "*O house of Israel*." This time the reference is less ironic and more poignant, an acknowledgment of their reality and how far they have fallen as a people.

Nephi then goes on to explain hard things that Israel will pass through. "[God] will also give [Nephi's people] for a light to the Gentiles." Nephi then adds a term in verse 8: "*O isles of the sea*." This is a new title embodying their current state and it is the opposite of what the house of Israel is. Here, Nephi is acknowledging reality. With this little addition he explains the exact situation they find

---

[231] Erez Ben-Yosef The Architectural Bias in Current Biblical Archaeology. In Vetus Testam. 69 (3), pp. 361–387. 2019

[232] It appears that Jacob (the brother of Nephi) reminds the people that they are infact of the house of Israel, "for ye are of the house of Israel." 2 Nephi 6:5

themselves in. Nephi explains why this is happening and assures his listeners that it will be temporary.

The talk then turns to the gathering of Israel. The refugees hear the words, *"house of Israel"* again in verse 12. After being called "isles of the sea," "house of Israel" may serve to remind Nephi's people that despite their current state they are *still* somehow the great house of Israel. Additionally, now used perhaps as a rhythmic device, the term likely serves to remind them their earlier poignant feelings. Nephi then may have paused as his listeners pondered on how they can be *both* the house of Israel and isles of the sea. Nephi continued, "Behold, these shall come from far; and lo, these from the north and from the west and these from the land of Sinim." Nephi's people likely understand this as a reference to the gathering of Israel. Are people truly being gathered back to Zion? Nephi then says, "Sing, O heavens; and be joyful, O earth;" Joyful singing is probably hard to imagine given the tragic state of things—what in the world is there to be joyful for? Why would the whole earth rejoice? Nephi then adds this phrase, *"for the feet of those who are in the east shall be established."* Nephi clarifies that this is not a reference to Judah's return from Babylon by adding, *"for they shall be smitten no more."* [233] This is Jerusalem's second return. That is why *his* people can rejoice: the return of the Jews is a sign that the Nephite and Lamanite exile is at an

---

[233] I will point out here that the interpretation of the passage does not depend on whether the author is Nephi or Isaiah. For example, from the frame of reference that Isaiah wrote the words, Professor Bruce Satterfield still considers that "those who are in the east" refers to Judah. See Bruce Satterfield, "ISAIAH 49 (1 NEPHI 21)," Brigham Young University, accessed September 11, 2022, https://emp.byui.edu/SATTERFIELDB/papers/Isaiah%2049.html.

end.[234] It appears Nephi has told his people what Isaiah's words mean with respect to their new position and given additional signs relevant to their new perspective. When Nephi's people see those return to Jerusalem the second time (for they shall be smitten no more), then is the time for all of Israel's gathering (including theirs), and thus they have reason to sing. Even the mountains are singing. All of this of course seems too good to be true; it is in fact the exact opposite of the reality in which they find themselves. Aware of their feelings and future difficulties, Nephi continues, "Zion hath said: The Lord hath forsaken me, and my Lord hath forgotten me." Then Nephi adds *"but he will show you that he hath not."* Nephi then reads one of the most powerful scriptures, describing the love the Savior has for us. Citing God, Nephi says, "For can a woman forget her sucking child, that she should not have compassion on the son of her womb? Yea, they may forget, yet will I not forget thee. *O house of Israel."* In this context the final, *"house of Israel"* references the *opposite* of what it did at the beginning of this passage. Instead of emphasizing what Nephi's people lost, the term is affirming. It tells them of God's love and *looks forward* to what they will become. They are the house of Israel and therefore God's power will bless them. God has promised their redemption and restoration. They are loved. Things will be okay and there is a sign to know what to look forward to.

In my view this is a beautiful and strengthening acknowledgement of the past, the present reality and the future. In this way Nephi gives knowledge and comfort to

---

[234] Namely the establishment of Judah - 2 Nephi 25:16-18.

his people. I believe Nephi uses his own words to weave them into Isaiah's words to emphasize the sure redemption they will feel, while still referencing their current hardships and being careful not to minimize their struggles. Nephi's declared a purpose and a plan. He did this that they may "lift up their hearts and rejoice…" [235]

Part of my purpose in writing about this passage is to appreciate Nephi's writing. I also want to demonstrate the importance of identifying high-fidelity and paraphrastic citations. We cannot know for certain which pieces of this passage Nephi counts as likening, or even what changes are his. However, Nephi seems to:

- Weave terms and allusions in with the current text
- Change the frame of reference from which the scripture is understood
- Give an additional prophecy or sign based on the new situation
- Juxtapose the current situation with the past, and future
- Juxtapose opposing emotions and experiences
- Use repetition and metric devices

If this altogether is what is meant by likening the scriptures (and I am not sure it is), we have a great work that lays before us. Nephi instructs all to liken the scriptures.

Repetition of the term, "*house of Israel*" may seem trivial to some as it does not seem to add new doctrine or information. But Alan Goff wrote repeated elements such as the term 'House of Israel' here, "aren't failures or shortcomings but are themselves artistic clues to narrative

---

[235] 2 Nephi 11:8

meaning that call readers to appreciate the depth of the story understood against the background of allusion and tradition. Adaptation and repetition are what Hebraic prophecy and narrative are about."[236]

Conclusion

Nephi tells us that he wrote his books words so his people could rejoice. The Nephite populace who experienced the unnerving loss of civilization upon leaving Jerusalem and whose typical daily worries included existential threats could put their minds at rest and know with surety that God lives, loves them, and has a plan.

The Nephite's use of both paraphrastic and high-fidelity citations appears to be a deliberate rhetorical tactic, adapted to highly personalized situations. With the knowledge of the applicable locution, one can posit which sections of text Nephi has modified. The techniques shown in 1 Nephi 21 are some of the tools the Nephites used to confront reality.

---

[236] Alan Goff, "Types of Repetition and Shadows of History in Hebraic Narrative," *Interpreter: A Journal of Latter-day Saint Faith and Scholarship* 45 (2021): 263–318.

Manufactured by Amazon.ca
Acheson, AB